exploring

DRAWING *for* ANIMATION

exploring

DRAWING *for*
ANIMATION

Kevin Hedgpeth
and Stephen Missal

THOMSON ™

DELMAR LEARNING

Australia Canada Mexico Singapore Spain United Kingdom United States

THOMSON

™

DELMAR LEARNING

Exploring Drawing for Animation
Kevin Hedgpeth and Stephen Missal

Vice President, Technology and Trades SBU:
Alar Elken

Editorial Director:
Sandy Clark

Acquisitions Editor:
James Gish

Development Editor:
Jaimie Wetzel

Marketing Director:
Cindy Eichelman

Channel Manager:
Fair Huntoon

Marketing Coordinator:
Sarena Douglass

Production Director:
Mary Ellen Black

Production Manager:
Larry Main

Production Editor:
Thomas Stover

Art/Design Coordinator:
Rachel Baker

Technology Project Manager:
David Porush

Editorial Assistant:
Marissa Maiella

Library of Congress
Cataloging-in-Publication Data:

Hedgpeth, Kevin.
   Exploring drawing for animation / Kevin Hedgpeth and Stephen Missal.
      p. cm.
Includes index.
   ISBN 1-4018-2419-6
   1. Animated films--Technique.   I. Missal, Stephen. II. Title.
   NC1765.H35 2003
   741.5'8--dc21

                                    2003008885

NOTICE TO THE READER

table of contents

table of contents

exploring drawing for animation

preface

INTENDED AUDIENCE

One of the absolute key requirements to success as an animator, whether in traditional 2D or computer animation, is good drawing technique. Despite some novice's claims that drawing skill is not important because of computer innovation, our experience and the experience of all major and minor studios involved in animation is that drawing is crucial. *Exploring Drawing for Animation* is expressly designed to show how drawing—in particular, life drawing—provides the foundation for understanding and creating animation. Also covered as part of this foundational skill set are sections on how to draw animals, human (and some animal) anatomy, and architecture and natural settings, as they are approached in mastering drawing techniques. This book is intended for use by professional animation schools, traditional college programs where animation is a part of the curriculum, and all drawing curricula, in general, where students may potentially follow up their initial studies with concentration in animation or by transferring to programs that teach animation, both traditional and computer generated. This text can also be used by professionals as a tool to help train novice animators or interns, and can even be useful outside of the school environment by an individual.

EMERGING TRENDS

As the animation market evolves, we have seen the emerging importance of computer-generated imagery and computer-related skills becoming more important. Traditional animation has moved strongly toward the advertising industry and television entertainment markets. The game industry now generates more income than the film industry, and we expect this trend to continue. Although the job market may be fluid and shift to wherever the predominant needs are felt, it is still a field where the need for foundational study and competence are vital. As these trends unfold, the skills acquired from traditional drawing and related studies will produce the designers and production artists of the future. Despite the interest in computer-based animation, the need for strong draftsmanship and design skills has not lessened; in fact, it may be more important than ever as a balance to slapdash or shoddy craftsmanship in either computer or traditional animation.

BACKGROUND OF THIS TEXT

Developing drawing skill is possible for just about anyone; all that is needed is a roadmap, so to speak. What has been missing in the instructional literature is a book tying drawing skills, as they are developed in a general sense, to animation as a field. We have filled the gap with this book As animation weaves more extensively into the information/communication, forensics, entertainment, and advertising fields, skills described and developed in our text will help to give the initial "glue" that will bind inspiration to production. This text describes in detail the theory and practice of drawing in a way that will enhance all potential animation venues.

The authors began the text with utilization of their own professional experience. Their combined history of professional animation, illustration, and college teaching reaches back several decades. As instructors at The Art Institute of Phoenix, a school dedicated to producing professionals in animation and other related fields, the authors have first-hand knowledge of the needs and paths necessary to success in this field. In addition, they have had discussions with professional animators from Fox Animation Studio and other professional artists in this field, including some who worked on *The Lord of the Rings* movie series. They have also researched and learned tips from major animation texts, and realize how those texts fall short in this area.

As a prerequisite, the student need only have the desire to pursue this path and a computer program within which to utilize this text. Several specific areas of education also need to be mastered by beginning and continuing professional animators. Many computer programs are available to the animator, especially in the computer-aided arena. Texts giving medical-level training about anatomy are also available. This book is a pre-program, so to speak, and would be considered generically text friendly. It is valuable because it goes back to the origins of many of the concepts found in other programs and books.

TEXTBOOK ORGANIZATION

This book is organized into nine chapters, along with some extra sections devoted to color reproductions of artwork related to the text and profiles of famous animators, both past and present. All chapters are profusely illustrated with artwork relating specifically to the subject being covered. Chapter 1 begins with an overview and primer on basic drawing skills. In Chapter 2, the connection between the quick sketch and more finished line drawings is made. This is related specifically to the needs of animation. Chapter 3 introduces anatomy in humans and some animals; it is intended as both a resource and a bridge between drawing skills discussed in the first two chapters and the skill sets presented in Chapter 4. This chapter is devoted to sequential drawing, where a series of quick, analytical sketches are tied together to investigate movement and anatomy. We move from quick sequential sketching to the nature of dramatic action and its relationship to living creatures in Chapter 5. At this point, the student will find numerous color images in the center section. These pieces of artwork demonstrate more finalized problem solving in layouts, drawing, and character and background design. Chapter 6 follows with specific issues involving architecture and scenery as they relate to drawing. Character design and development, the next chapter, introduces ways and means of creating characters, and the pitfalls, resource issues, and drawing solutions to various themes. Further development of this theme culminates in Chapter 8, where style, exaggeration, and realism get coverage. The use of the model sheet also is introduced here. Finally, Chapter 9 goes into character layout, rough animation, and cleanup for animation, as they are related to drawing, in general. A section that interviews two professional animators and cleanup artists concludes the book. Key points throughout the text are printed in italic type, allowing for easy identification by teacher and student alike. Although some technical information concerning animations is covered in the last chapter, our intention was mainly to show how this is a natural outcome of learning foundational drawing skills.

FEATURES

- Objectives clearly state the learning goals of each chapter.
- Illustrations are used generously to enhance the concepts learned.
- Profiles of successful animation give important history and industry advice.
- Foundational skills in drawing and their theory are covered extensively in a user-friendly manner.
- The relationship between quick or gesture drawing and successful animation is examined in depth.
- Anatomical information is covered thoroughly in a practical manner; general guides are given for drawing each gender.

HOW TO USE
THIS TEXT

The following features can be found
throughout this book:

▶ ## Objectives

Learning Objectives start off each
chapter. They describe the com-
petencies the readers should
achieve upon understanding
the chapter material.

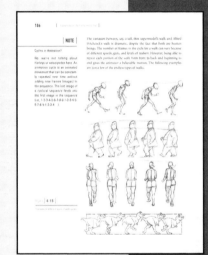

▶ ## Notes

Notes provide special hints, practical
techniques, and information to
the reader.

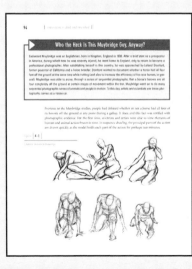

▶ ## Sidebars

Sidebars appear
throughout the text,
offering additional
valuable information
on specific topics.

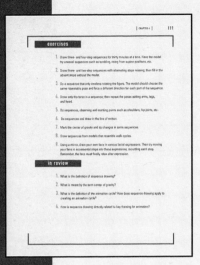

Review Questions and Exercises

Review Questions and Exercises are located at the end of each chapter and allow the reader to assess their understanding of the chapter. Exercises are intended to reinforce chapter material through practical application.

The Animator at Work

These career profiles are interspersed throughout the text. Each features a successful animator in the field.

Get Creative

The creative process is important for anyone in an artistic field to understand. These articles are included to help the reader understand how to tap into their creativity and get their creative juices flowing.

about the authors

▶ Kevin Hedgpeth

Kevin Hedgpeth is an Assistant Academic Director in the animation and game art programs at The Art Institute of Phoenix. He also teaches a number of animation classes, as well. Kevin is an Animation Consultant for the Puppeteers of America, Inc. and an ASIFA Central member. The official logo for National Day of Puppetry 2001 was his creation. Kevin has worked as an illustrator and designer for games, toy and animation properties with Myers Entertainment Group, and has experience as a professional stop-motion animator for television advertising. He is also the author of a profile of Miyazaki in *Shade* magazine, and is collaborating with several colleagues on animation projects at the Art Institute. Educated at Arizona State University, Kevin makes his home in Phoenix, Arizona, where he actively pursues a dual career as artist and educator/author.

▶ Stephen Missal

Stephen Missal is also an instructor at the Art Institute of Phoenix. His background starts with an education at Wichita State University, where he earned his Masters degree. An educator for thirty years, Stephen also has a long professional history of showings in galleries, where many of his paintings and drawings have been sold nationally. Among significant collections his work has been included in are Frank Sinatra, Itzhak Perlman, Gary Owens, and the New Britain Museum of American Art. As an illustrator, his work has been utilized by such companies as Wizards of the Coast, Winchester Press, Gorsuch/Scarisbrick Press, Arizona Public Service, and Salt River Project. He adjudicates art competitions frequently, and is now adding book author to his activities.

Both authors are H. P. Lovecraft devotees, and while Kevin fancies gorilla images for his personal icon, Stephen thinks that squids and octopi are essential to happiness.

INSTRUCTOR'S GUIDE ON CD-ROM

The Instructor's Guide on CD-ROM is a great resource for instructors. It contains sample syllabi for using this book in either an 11- or 15-week course. It provides answers to the review questions found in the text, tips for assessing completed exercises assigned in the book, and a list of additional resources. It also includes PowerPoint slides that highlight main topics and frame classroom discussion.

Order # 1-4018-7870-9

ACKNOWLEDGMENTS

The authors would like to acknowledge the following people for their invaluable help in writing this text. First are their parents and patient spouses and children, who endured endless rewrites and drawing sessions. Terrance Yee, instructor at the Art Institute of Phoenix and a fine, nationally recognized illustrator, provided much information and inspiration. Cesar Avalos and Andrzej Piotrowski—fine artists, animators, and instructors at the Art Institute of Phoenix—helped fill in crucial blanks in our story, and were patient enough to sit for interviews. Ray Harryhausen is remembered as an inspiration and creative muse for both Kevin and Stephen. Finally, but by no means least, we wish to thank the editors at Delmar Learning, especially Jaimie Wetzel. Her patience and good humor both guided and calmed the authors' written journey and occasional hysteria.

Delmar Learning and the authors would also like to thank the following reviewers for their valuable suggestions and technical expertise:

MAR ELEPANO
School of Cinema and Television
University of Southern California
Los Angeles, California

LEE LANIER
Media Arts and Animation Department
Art Institute of Las Vegas
Las Vegas, Nevada

ROBERT EPPS
Animation Department
International School of Design and Technology
Tampa, Florida

E. ANNE PENNINGTON
Graphic Design Department
College of the Sequoias
Visalia, California

BERNEY KRULE
Chair, Graphic Design Department
Oakton Community College
Des Plaines, Illinois

QUESTIONS AND FEEDBACK

Delmar Learning and the authors welcome your questions and feedback. If you have suggestions that you think others would benefit from, please let us know and we will try to include them in the next edition.

To send us your questions and/or feedback, you can contact the publisher at:

DELMAR LEARNING

Executive Woods

5 Maxwell Drive

Clifton Park, NY 12065

Attn: Graphic Arts Team

800-998-7498

Or the authors at:

KEVIN HEDGPETH

c/o The Art Institute of Phoenix

2233 W. Dunlap Avenue

Phoenix, AZ 85021

602-678-4300

STEPHEN MISSAL

c/o The Art Institute of Phoenix

2233 W. Dunlap Avenue

Phoenix, AZ 85021

602-678-4300

introduction

DRAWING FOR ANIMATION

There are many excellent books available as an introduction to two- and three-dimensional animation for the student. So why do we need another one? In all the texts available, there are none that thoroughly address the issue of drawing, especially life drawing, as it relates to and helps define animation. Some books are specialized volumes, concerned only with general animation principles, or are purely fundamental drawing books, or are confined only to life drawing. These subjects taken alone can be difficult for a beginning student to integrate into a useable technique. We have gathered these subjects into an introductory form, and related their uses in such a way that a student starting the journey into the world of animation can more quickly learn and adapt them to various projects. It is highly suggested that anyone learning to draw and animate should acquire a large collection of reference materials dealing with all of the above-mentioned subjects; we make no pretence at being exhaustive in any area. What we have done is to tie techniques together in a way unique to this burgeoning field. By observing the illustrations and trying out the exercises at the end of each chapter, the student should find the field of animation less obscure and considerably more fun. In the text, some words are in italic type; we intend these to be key thoughts or points to be focused on by the student and teacher. They often summarize a larger segment of the book or illustrate key ideas. In conjunction with the illustrations, we hope that many of the mysteries of drawing, especially as it relates to animations, will become clearer.

What students will find as they progress in this field is that drawing skill and knowledge related to drawing are integral to their success. Over and over, we have been told—and have witnessed first-hand with our own students—the direct connection between drawing skills and first-rate animators. This includes special effects and background artists, as well. At first, drawing can be intimidating for those with a limited background to learn. But as they progress, it becomes addictive, as does the animating itself. The only limits really are hard work and time. So good luck, turn the pages, and give it a try!

solid drawing

objectives

Develop an understanding of fundamental drawing skills and how to acquire them

Discover the relationship of drawing skill to animation

Use proportional measuring tools

Gather an understanding of rendering techniques for drawing

Learn to apply line technique to animation and drawing

Gain knowledge of the concept of the quick sketch/gesture drawing

introduction

Good drawing skills necessary for animation are no different from the skills needed for basically sound drawing from life. In that book of inestimable importance to animators *The Illusion of Life: Disney Animation*, one of the "12 Principles of Animation" is solid drawing. Solid drawing refers to the ability of the animator to create figures that have weight, solidity, depth, and balance: a drawing that appears to be three-dimensional. The ability to draw well is the cornerstone of two-dimensional (2D) animation.

Even if an artist has no intention of working in the traditional animation field, the techniques put forth in this chapter are both universal and invaluable. The uses for good technique go into many areas. For example: character development, rough storyboards, concept development, backgrounds, key-framing, and in-betweening in traditional animation; all these and more rely on a strong ability to draw. Somewhere, somehow, no matter what final means are used to produce the animation, there must be some artist scribbling down ideas in visual form. Success in this field greatly depends on this skill finding its way into the final product. Remember: weak art equals unsuccessful animation.

If we become dependent upon software programs for designing, we will limit ourselves. Integrating drawing-by-hand skills with computer technology will always give us the greatest number of options as designers.

Throughout this book, we have inserted some fun, extra information and have indicated important points with italicized type. Look for these pointers as you read, and pay careful attention to the visual examples that illustrate each one.

SOLID DRAWING

STARTING OUT

Any quick survey of current literature in drawing instruction will produce many examples of valid and time-tested techniques. You can and should look at many of these in order to increase your abilities. Within the confines of this book, there are a number of techniques and methodologies that have proven themselves over the several decades of teaching between the two authors. Quite frankly, simple is best for any method. None of us has the time to memorize the reams of data available, but there are a few, very easy-to-remember facts and methods that will aid you well when you are struggling with drawing. We will present these as the chapter unfolds.

Like anything else, to get good at something you have to practice doing it a lot. That is a simplistic way of addressing the toughest obstacle in learning to draw, the "no-brainer" part: do a lot of drawing. Draw from life and take figure-drawing classes as often as possible. Keep a sketchbook to record ideas and draw from your surroundings. Copy art and artist's styles that you admire. These are tried and true methods; we would add that it also helps to have a competent teacher available for feedback.

RELAXING, OR IT'S <u>NOT</u> ALL IN THE WRIST

Drawing for animation requires a strong ability to do what are called *gesture drawings* (also known as quick sketches, scribble drawings, etc.). It is advisable that you learn to relax your drawing hand and get off the point of the drawing tool in order to be successful at creating these drawings.

figure | 1-1 |

Natural hand position for drawing.

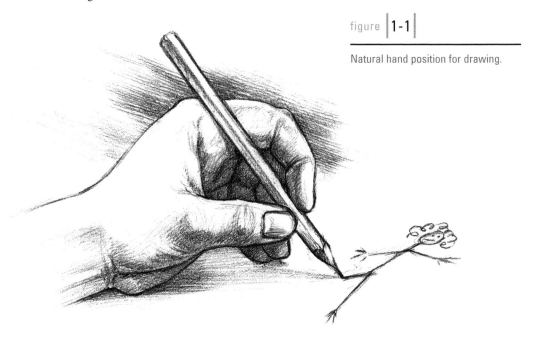

The reason for this is that natural wrist, arm, and hand motions combined will produce the types of curves and lines necessary to construct the varied forms encountered in character design and animation. These larger "motions" are more efficient than using just the fingers to produce even curves rapidly, long straight lines for architectural backgrounds, and oblongs and similar closed forms used to build more complex objects. The more vertical the drawing tool, the more pressure and drag on the page. This slows down the action and allows the line to wander from its intended course.

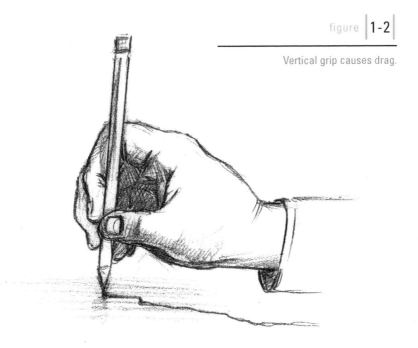

figure | 1-2 |

Vertical grip causes drag.

Although you may not be able to adopt a new grip on a pencil/charcoal/pen, you may be able to compensate in other ways by at least being aware of how your grip and hand motion affect the drawing.

Commonly used tools for drawing include graphite pencils (these come in various grades of hardness; softer 8B through 2B having more graphite and less clay; H through 6H having more clay than graphite), charcoal sticks and pencils (in soft, medium, and hard grades), pens (such as dipping pen points like crow-quill or mechanical pens that have ink cartridges and several sizes of points), Conté crayons (a soft chalk-like substance), and pastels. Pencils and materials that come in stick form can be held in two ways (as seen in figures 1-2 and 1-3).

NOTE

Drawing is a physical activity. We tend to think of it as more mental or creative, and these certainly play their part, but drawing actually requires some common sense positioning and movement. First, sit upright. Any slouching will put stress on the neck and upper back muscles, causing the inevitable discomfort and wandering attention. If you are using a drawing bench, place the drawing board under the pad of paper such that the board rests on your knees, not on the bench. This provides a better and more comfortable angle for the arm and hand. Otherwise the wrist is bent to accommodate the sharper angle, and this is tiring for the artist. Don't rotate your wrist "in" as you draw. If you do, the wrist is locked and all motions must come from the shoulder, which does allow great curves but is poor for smaller motions. Allow the wrist to remain in a more natural position, similar to reaching out and shaking someone's hand. If you are at a desk or drawing table, sit far enough above the drawing to allow good movement and to avoid distortion visually from top to bottom. Tilt the table if you can. The arc of the wrist motion is given freer rein if the grip is not down at the point, but further up the pencil. This also gives the artist a better view of their drawing in progress because the hand is not in the way.

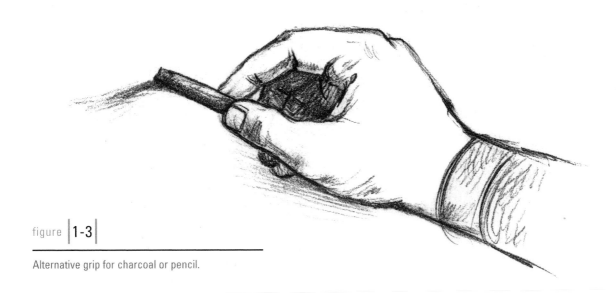

figure | 1-3 |

Alternative grip for charcoal or pencil.

Each grip has its place. The close grip similar to writing has tight control, and the more open grip is useful for large layouts. Remember, try to keep the wrist from rotating over so that there is no freedom left in the wrist. Confining yourself to mechanical pencils can rob you of the type of line quality available in softer and broader leads and sticks, which are useful for more dynamic, partly rendered drawings commonly found in the preliminary work in the animation industry. For tighter, closely rendered studies of anatomical items and mechanical contrivances, the small lead found in mechanical pencils can be used to great success.

Try a variety of drawing tools, but start out with the tool that is the most comfortable for you to handle successfully and progress from there.

figure | 1-4 |

Mechanical pencil.

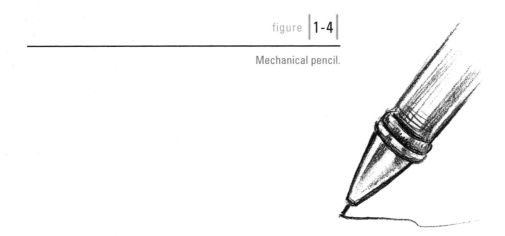

ONE SIZE DOES NOT FIT ALL

Proportional drawing remains the great "bugaboo" for all developing artists.

There are a good many texts available that address basic measuring techniques. What is really practical, however, is a system that is easily recalled at any time. The following is a very simple system that has worked for years for the authors in many college classes.

When we draw from life, most of us plunge in intuitively, sampling a bit of the image at a time, hoping that as we add one part to another that eventually the object will emerge on the page. The problem with this is that the brain doesn't like to keep track of so many separate bits of visual information. Scale, placement, and spatial orientation are lost in the shuffle, as one part starts at an initial scale and the final part is at an entirely different scale. Time can be wasted while adjusting one fragment of the drawing to match another. In this case, the sum of all parts is not greater than the whole! All artists have experienced this frustration. But, there are a few simple techniques and rules that can help you to avoid this catastrophe. *"Draw what you*

figure 1-5

Bugaboo: "An object of obsessive, usually exaggerated fear or anxiety," rendered for you here in its rarely seen corporeal form. (Special thanks to *The American Heritage Dictionary, 4th Edition,* for this definition.)

see, not what you think *you see*" tops the list. In other words, depend on your eyes for all visual information. Preconceived notions about what something *should* look like will cripple your efforts. Stylistic exaggeration should come later, after you have mastered actual life drawing. Some teachers recommend distorting the figure for emotive or genre-driven reasons, but this prevents you from learning how to accurately determine basic visual information. Even Picasso started out as a master draftsman before he veered off into Cubism and other styles. Picasso *learned* the rules before he *broke* the rules.

Another rule that will greatly improve life drawing is: Big before small, simple before complex. This is probably the most crucial of all the actual physical techniques. It has to do with how we can record, quickly and in a kind of visual shorthand, anything in front of us. There are several different approaches to this type of drawing. *Gesture drawings,* or quick sketches— simple diagrammatic versions of the object being drawn—are done in a variety of styles and are the most effective means of translating the three-dimensional object into a two-dimensional drawing with the most important information intact. In some styles, an imaginary line running through the axis (line) of motion or action leads the early process of drawing the figure. This *line of action* indicates the dominant direction of action as it "flows" through the figure, often centering on the spine or centerline.

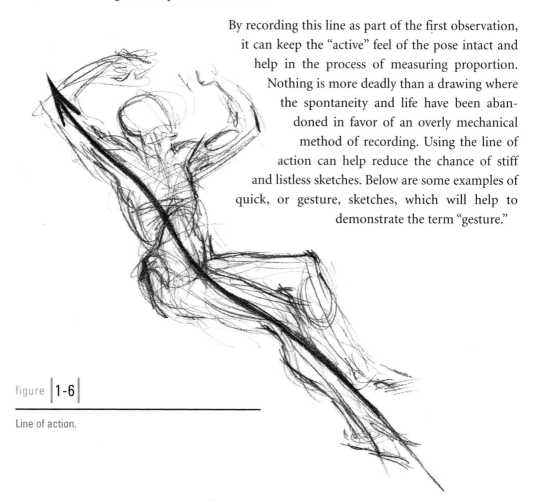

By recording this line as part of the first observation, it can keep the "active" feel of the pose intact and help in the process of measuring proportion. Nothing is more deadly than a drawing where the spontaneity and life have been abandoned in favor of an overly mechanical method of recording. Using the line of action can help reduce the chance of stiff and listless sketches. Below are some examples of quick, or gesture, sketches, which will help to demonstrate the term "gesture."

figure |1-6|

Line of action.

Trying out some of these styles is an excellent means of learning to create a viable style of your own. Remember, a gesture sketch is just a means to an end (your final rendered drawing) and is not intended to be "beautiful" or finished looking. What else is part of a gesture drawing? We can include some anatomy, such as a hint of the skeletal framework and some of the major muscle groups to create volume. By combining these elements with "action" lines and extra construction lines, the artist can give both life and initial accuracy to a drawing. Make sure that your gestural line-work is not arbitrary; you are building structure! It is not recommended that you "plot" out major measuring points, or start with a stiff "stick-man."

figures |1-7| and |1-8|

Gesture sketches.

| NOTE |

Most beginners are afraid of the look of loose, preliminary drawings. They are, to a certain extent, nervous that their peers or other critical audiences will make fun of such an unpolished look in a gesture or quick preliminary sketch. The truth is, you have to ignore layman comments and trust in this technique. Being a professional is not for the faint of heart, and facing criticism is uncomfortable. All great draftsmen utilize this method with success, and you can, too.

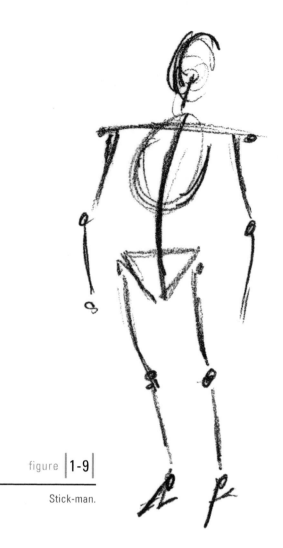

figure | 1-9 |

Stick-man.

These will surely fossilize your technique. Don't worry about small visual information; it can always be added later. What is needed is large, simple information, because proportion and action are what are ultimately going to make or break the drawing. Remember that a gesture drawing is a quick sketch that describes the basic movement and volume of the figure.

Frequently, several parts of a figure can be combined to make a larger shape.

You will notice that there are open poses and closed poses, and poses having both traits. An open pose, such as a running one, clearly is spread out from the center torso area, whereas the closed pose tends to have more overlapping and a more simplistic overall silhouette.

Open, closed and combined poses,
with combined areas.

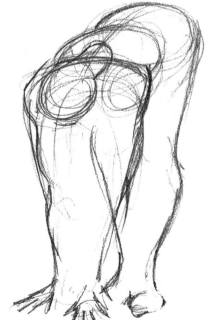

We will touch more on this later, but it is obvious that the type of pose will affect the way in which we draw the figure. Loose is better in this scenario. As the artist moves from place to place on the figure, a more continuous line "sculpts" the form as it is drawn, as well as keeps the brain/attention engaged by a continuous kinesthetic feedback. That is, as the arm and eyes move, they interact with what is being produced on the page, and this back and forth input modifies the next action the artist takes in the drawing. In the next chapter we will explore gesture drawings in more detail, with an eye to types and styles of quick sketching appropriate to different circumstances.

PROPORTION, OR WHY ART SEEMS SO MYSTERIOUS

What is proportion? Remember, when we draw from life (or even our imagination) we are translating three dimensions onto two (your flat piece of paper or illustration board). The paper we draw on is a version of an imaginary plane of glass that intersects the image as it is transmitted from the object to our eye.

figure | 1-12

Image projected onto imaginary picture plane.

This is an arbitrary "cut-off" of the image; we can see that as the image gets closer to the eye, its scale diminishes to almost nothing as it enters the pupil. Proportion is this image, if you will: an accurate perspective rendition of a three-dimensional object. We know that this "glass" image is by and large what our eye sees. The glass, being at right angles to our line of sight, prevents distortion due to anamorphic projection (extreme elongation).

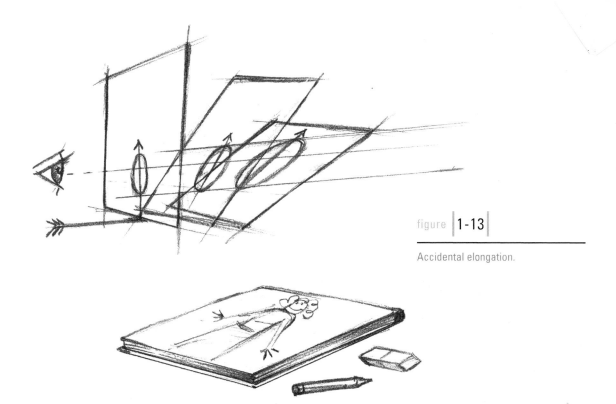

figure | 1-13 |

Accidental elongation.

This is why drawing on a flat surface, although tempting, is not a good idea. There is a high likelihood of vertical elongation. Since carting around planes of glass is about as convenient as ice-skating on gravel, artists use a substitute (a handy pad of paper). Proportion is the sum of measurements that is equal to the image accuracy. To put it simply, proportion is whether your hand-produced image visually matches what you see. What particular things can we actually measure? If you look at an image traced on a pane of glass, you will notice that it is flat. In other words, we can measure in two directions: up/down and left/right.

figure | 1-14 |

Measuring on a flat surface.

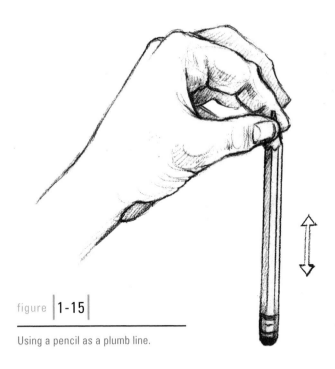

figure **1-15**

Using a pencil as a plumb line.

These measurements refer to vertical and horizontal in the "real" world, where true vertical is relative to gravity. You can use your pencil as a plumb line to find vertical, and by then moving your hand at right angles to this pencil you will locate horizontal.

When drawing on a pad of paper, the top and bottom of the pad are parallel to horizontal, and the left and right edges are parallel to vertical. So our pad of paper is a miniature "version" of the world we are drawing. By noting this, *you will realize immediately that any measurement in the actual world has a corresponding measurement on the paper.* Each measurement (real world and pad of paper) moves in this up/down and left/right mode. The qualities that can be measured are direction (angle of lean), size, and relative position. In addition, shape can be inferred from these observations. No matter how else you think about it, measuring reduces down to these few simple principles. We have codified these concepts into the "A.S.P." system, or:

- A - Angle
- S - Size
- P - Position

Within this system, we also use a "crutch," or backup tool for when the drawing isn't working just right. This we call *home base* (HB), which is some area in our drawing that can be easily measured and returned to for reference when things go badly elsewhere in the sketch. This will be discussed in greater detail later.

Angle refers to the direction of any long axis of an object in relation to vertical and/or horizontal. A long axis is an imaginary line running through the length of an object (or part of an object, such as an arm). A circle is one of the few cases where there can be no long axis. The short axis (across the width of the object) is not very useful to artists and is left out of this system. The long axis can be matched by holding a pencil *along* the axis and comparing this measurement to vertical or horizontal elements. You merely hold your pencil in between your eye and what you are measuring, keeping the pencil parallel to that imaginary picture plane in front of you, and align the pencil with any two points or any long axis. Because you are drawing on a flat surface, there is no need to *point* the pencil in or out (toward or away from you). You measure as though you were butted up against a huge color print, instead of three-dimensional space.

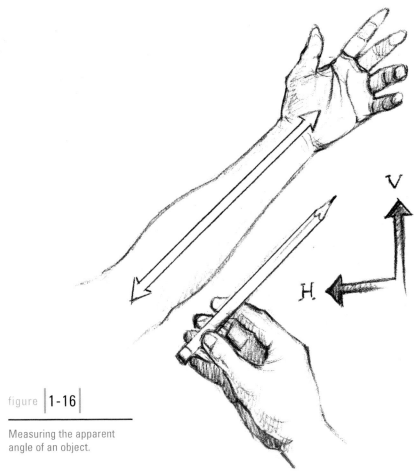

figure |1-16|

Measuring the apparent
angle of an object.

With practice, the artist can produce accuracy
within a degree or so using this simple device.
Almost anything can be measured in this way:
a nose, an eye, a tree limb, and so forth. Even
irregular shapes yield a general direction that
can be verified this way.

Another quality that we see in the world is relative size. One very important aspect of visual
information that affects measuring size is *foreshortening*. What is foreshortening? In referring
back to our pane of glass tracing, we see that
although in actual three-dimensional space
objects can move away from us or toward us
with their long axis, on the pane of glass all is
flat, and these foreshortened forms become

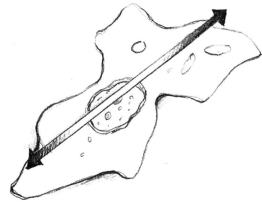

figure |1-17|

Irregular objects can have direction.

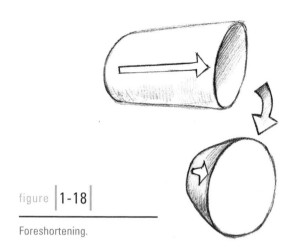

figure |1-18|

Foreshortening.

merely abbreviated shapes like ovals and such. Foreshortening refers to this change of drawn shape when the long axis of a form is no longer parallel to the picture plane.

Thus, when someone points an arm and hand toward you, the drawn shape on your pad of paper no longer looks like what your mind thinks of as the "real" shape of an arm or hand. This is the moment of truth, so to speak. Our "standard" image pulled from recognition signals in the brain does not match the odd shape now revealed to us visually. As a result, we force our preconceived image onto what we see, and amazingly, will draw what is in our memory and not what is in front of us. That is why so many teachers say: draw what you see, not what you think you see. Foreshortening produces abstract shapes on the imaginary picture plane. We understand the objects as we look at them in real space, but when they are projected as flat, foreshortened shapes, our brain wrestles with the unfamiliar.

We must take the *size* of an object or part of an object into consideration when we draw it. An easy (and ancient) method for measuring relative size is as follows: using a pencil (or other long drawing tool), held at arm's length from your body, locate one end of the part you wish to measure with the end of the pencil, and then mark the other end of this part with your thumb. Close one eye as you do this to prevent the distortion arising from the phenomena of parallax in binocular vision; that is, mixing the images of both eyes.

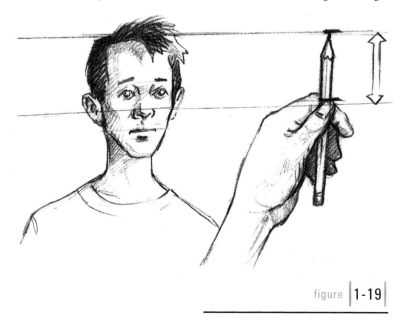

Make sure to keep your arm fully extended when measuring objects in this fashion to avoid changing scale. This little "piece" of the object will become your yardstick, a repeatable unit that can measure in every direction (on the imaginary pane of glass). So, this exercise helps to explain what the terms "six heads tall" or "three arm-lengths long" mean. We are merely showing a relative measurement; that is, how many of these units make up larger parts of the object. All of these measure-

figure |1-19|

Measuring relative size using a pencil.

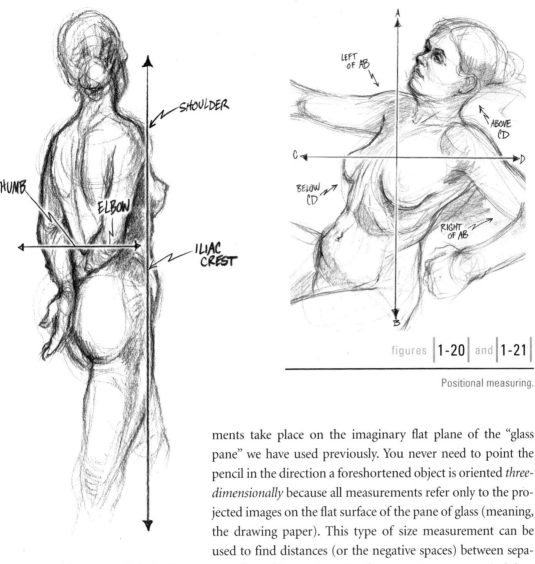

figures **1-20** and **1-21**

Positional measuring.

ments take place on the imaginary flat plane of the "glass pane" we have used previously. You never need to point the pencil in the direction a foreshortened object is oriented *three-dimensionally* because all measurements refer only to the projected images on the flat surface of the pane of glass (meaning, the drawing paper). This type of size measurement can be used to find distances (or the negative spaces) between separate objects, as well. Using larger parts of an object as the unit of measure is more practical than using smaller parts; there are fewer and more accurate measurements for the artist to make.

The final ingredient to A.S.P. is *position. Positional measuring merely refers to locating the relative position of two (or more) points on the imaginary picture plane by using angle and size.* We can locate things also by referring to an imaginary central line or axis to determine if it is left or right of this axis, or above or below it, depending on verticality or horizontality.

Another method is to drop a line straight down or directly left or right of one point to determine where another point is in relation to the first; that is, do they line up or not. Because of the overlap of one object or object-part over another, positional measurement becomes a crucial component of the proportion game. Once part of a drawing has been established, we can use this simple but effective shorthand method to locate numerous drawn elements in relation to each other. Without clearly understanding the relationship of the parts to each other, we can only do parts. All we would have is a jumble of small, accurate images.

Earlier, we introduced the idea of home base, a place in the drawing where measurements could be made with some surety to provide a place to refer to later. This area is usually larger and simpler than other areas, and has an easily determined angle. Often, as in the case of a torso, for example, the width versus the length can be at least visually estimated (or exactly measured if desired). This provides a "piece" that is, in and of itself, secure visually and in the context of the whole drawing.

Now this home base area can be used to determine the accuracy of the adjacent parts of the drawing, thus increasing the size of the accurately drawn area. By using this remeasurement process, the drawing can be rescued. It is not recommended that this be the only means of resurrecting a dying drawing, but under time pressure or with a lack of replacement material this method can be a lifesaver.

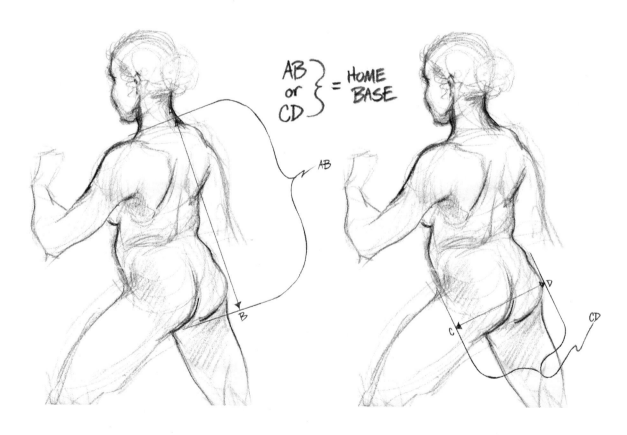

figure | 1-22 |

Human torso as home base.

figure |1-23|

Fifteen minute sketch.

Shape is an issue that has more to do with brain function than drawing technique. However, having said that, the use of larger hand, wrist, and arm motions will produce clean, relatively accurate lines, ovals, ellipses, and so forth that are quite practical in starting realistic forms. To reproduce that which is in front of us is simpler in some ways than we think. Small motions from the fingers give shaky, irregular forms that usually lack accuracy or quality. They are more suited to details than larger forms. Flicking the wrist outward can construct surprisingly straight lines. Using the shoulder's ball and socket motions can produce excellent ovals and ellipses. By drawing simple "preshapes" and modifying them with true measurements, we can achieve accurate shapes using very simple means.

Drawing, as we have said, is a physical activity. It involves small and large motion with the hand, fingers, wrist, elbow joint, and shoulder joint. Because the wrist allows a natural arc of motion, and the shoulder's ball and socket arrangement gives us a pendulum-like swing of the arm, anyone using these body movements can produce beautiful and useful curves, ovals, ellipses, and so on. This activity, done in a relaxed but controlled manner, through practice, becomes natural and preferred, leaving the smaller hand and finger motions reserved for detail.

Ultimately, most mistakes that crop up as a drawing progresses are the result of a few very simple measuring errors. If a torso leans too far in one direction, an inexperienced artist may unconsciously try to compensate by lengthening another part of the body, not realizing that this will merely compound the problem. So, the rule is: be certain of your initial, biggest measurements. Don't skip them. Intuition is a wonderful thing, but it cannot be relied upon for highly accurate drawings. If you are working under difficult conditions, remember that there is a fundamental set of techniques that can save the day. Do a rough sketch to begin with; *something* on the page is better than a blank page, and now you have something to work with. Draw simply and without detail.

Remember:

- Large things before small things; simple things before complex things.
- Be loose and free in your drawing.
- Any extra lines can always be removed by one of the great inventions of all time: the eraser.

Now, as you begin to tighten up the drawing, use A.S.P. to determine the accuracy of the large measurements. All small measurements depend upon large measurements, and so should be left alone until later. Be ruthless in your corrections. Any sloppiness or cutting corners merely reinforces bad habits that can be difficult to break. *Make sure to correct mistakes in your drawing completely.* Don't partially correct an element. Drawings can look pretty goofy during this process, but in the end, a polished product can result. Laymen viewing a drawing in progress might not understand what you are doing, but ignore their comments or suggestions, and don't worry if your drawing doesn't look "photo-real" from the start. It can look that way later, if that is what you wish. What is important is to follow the steps as previously outlined. The temptation to attempt a finished look from the beginning means a tedious, incredibly long effort that could produce the desired result in a fraction of the time with proper technique. All great artists, from the old masters like Rubens to contemporary animation artists like Glenn Keane (of Walt Disney Studios), utilize sound techniques much like those we've discussed in this chapter. We recommend following their fine examples.

LIGHT, DARK, AND RENDERING

Line drawings are inventions of the human mind. The reality around us does not appear as a simple, outlined cartoon strip, like the daily funnies. Instead, we comprehend it by means of value (light and dark), color, pattern, focus, and contextual judgment. As artists working in simple monochromatic (one-color) media, the value scale of light and dark applied to three-dimensional objects becomes a powerful tool to fool the viewer into believing that the drawn objects have actual weight and substance. The human eye can detect hundreds of differing values, but in practical application only five to ten are ever used in drawings. The reason for this is that our perceptual centers in the brain only require broad, simple value changes in order to recognize things in the world. As hunter/gatherers over the millennia, we have adapted to our own survival needs. A consequence of this is that, although we are quite sophisticated visually, quick and simple visual cues are all that are needed for recognition. So the hunter, looking for deer in the woods to feed a family, only needs enough clues to differentiate the deer from its surroundings in order to hunt it. In the same way, an artist can arouse a powerful recognition response from the viewer with simple, strong contrast value rendering; the need for detail is minimal. Although our conceptual mind desires or feels the need for excess detail to render reality, oddly enough, the opposite is true. How many times have you heard someone say, "This art is so detailed, it seems real"? This is a layman's response to art. If you tested them with a number of strongly rendered figure drawings, they would be surprised to discover that the ones that seemed most "real" were in fact drawn with a greater economy of means.

There are three main techniques for hand-producing light and dark effects in a drawing, as shown in Figure 1-24.

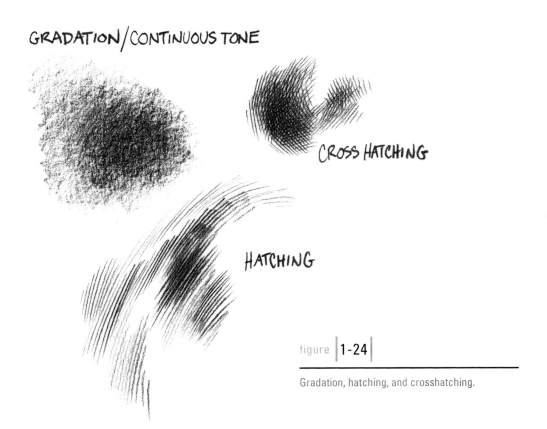

figure | 1-24 |

Gradation, hatching, and crosshatching.

The first, and simplest, is *gradation:* a smooth, nondirectional application of charcoal, Conté, graphite, or similar material to create continuous tone. By changing the pressure and applying over-layers, the artist can produce a wide variety of values and clean, controlled changes from one value to another.

This technique most nearly matches how our eye sees. Some artists use a stub or chamois to further rub the medium into extremely smooth gradations.

figure | 1-25

Illustration using gradation.

The second technique frequently used is *hatching*, a series of parallel lines of varying spacing, weight, and length that when combined produce a pleasing tonal effect in a drawing. Shorter strokes are more controllable, and the artist has the option of placing the strokes either in one direction (ala Leonardo da Vinci) or in a series of straight and curved groups of lines that travel in different directions as dictated by the form. The latter produces an almost topographical map sensation, but is technically more difficult to produce. It should be noted that these strokes have both thick ends and thin ends. This can cause a problem of excess value strips where they overlap when new bunches of hatching are added. To overcome this, an alternative application technique that can be used is the back-and-forth "slapping brush" method, where the strokes go in *two* directions instead of only one. By doing this, the fat and skinny ends average out visually and the result is a smooth-looking hatching technique. This is especially effective when rendering long, smooth hair or large surfaces.

Finally, the most commonly used technique is *crosshatching*, which is merely hatching taken in many different directions in an overlapping technique. Best success is seen with shorter strokes and multilayering. Density and numbers of overlapping hatched lines eventually determine the "darkness" or value of an area, with bits of hatching and crosshatching tapering off into lighter zones as transitional values. If the artist overlays the hatching layers at right angles, the result is a flatter look, which, unless stylistically called for, is to be avoided. Crosshatching is a somewhat slower technique, and should be reserved for occasions when there is a need and enough time. Often crosshatching is mixed with hatching (and even gradation) to produce a richer, variety-filled drawing. The danger, of course, is that the techniques, rather than complementing each other, will actually not "fit" together visually, and will instead distract the viewer from the unity of the image.

figure | 1-26 |

Problematic crosshatching.

Stippling is an additional technique used by many artists for rendering light and dark. We will not dwell on stippling too much as it is a slow, tedious technique not well suited to sketching and animation application. An example of stippling (multidot technique) is shown below. Note that again spacing, dot size, and weight produce the effects desired.

For an object to appear three-dimensional, it must have at least three values: light, dark, and a transitional middle value. The broader the value scale, the greater the drama and sense of real dimensionality will be. Many drawings suffer from tending toward one part of the scale or another, resulting in blandness or extreme light or dark areas. Utilizing a fuller value scale with

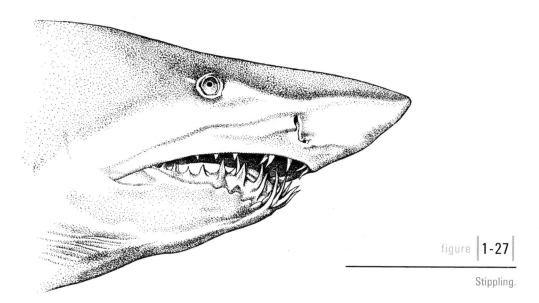

figure |1-27|

Stippling.

care can help you to avoid this problem. In creating character studies and backgrounds, the artist will realize the importance of just the right amount of contrast to solve the problem at hand. The ultimate goal is readability and clarity, along with style and dramatic considerations.

figure |1-28|

Scene with full value range or scale.

Another factor to consider is the type and direction of the light source. The classic sphere with a single light source and cast shadow demonstrates the most basic example of a rendered object/value scale.

figure | 1-29 |

Light-produced values on a sphere.

Reflected light can be used to good effect to help give the sensation of roundness. Remember that a reflected-light area is actually several steps darker than a highlighted area. In drawing for animation, rendered studies are of modest use only, more applicable to character development and backgrounds than anything else. Depending upon your goals, concentration on this area of technique may need to take a back seat to sketching and line techniques. With the advent of computer-generated imagery, it is still important, however, to understand the concept of value in creating modeled forms.

A WORD, OR A COUPLE HUNDRED, ON LINE

To produce useable line for sketching is not as simple as it might seem. This is partly due to the mechanics of how we hold the drawing instrument, and partly to our experience in producing the effect we want. In quick sketches, absolutely clean, beautiful line is not very important. However, readable line quality is still necessary. Those aspects of line that we should pay close attention to include thick and thinness, darkness, and cleanness (which is produced by quicker, more wrist/arm-initiated motion). The slower, finger techniques often leave small, wavering drawings that lack the punch and drama required for animation. Line itself, as we have said, actually does not exist in nature the way we use it. Its function for artists is to delineate structural changes and outlines by showing a silhouette boundary of form. These elements are critical in clean up for 2D animation. Although in fine arts there are many varieties of line quality that can describe different things and produce many pleasing styles, a simple approach is the best for the animator. *Extra lines that show up while sketching are not a problem; they are part of the process.* Although this introduction to line may seem brief, this topic is of great importance to the animator.

CHAPTER SUMMARY

Animation artists must understand the importance of practicing and becoming successful at the fundamental techniques of drawing, including visual measuring and tool use. Fundamental "mark-making" techniques (such as line and value-rendering methods) coupled with the artist's ability to comprehend and apply the concepts of observed proportion (as measured by angle, size, and position), act as a solid foundation for the creation of the gesture drawing. These basic drawing abilities then translate into the skill set required for quick sketching and its transition into animation drawing.

exercises

1. Using a pane of Plexiglas™, trace a scene or object. Then using this as a guide, draw the same scene or object freehand, comparing the two as you go.

2. With a pencil, measure the angles of as many long axes as you wish, then check these against traced angle measurements on the pane of Plexiglas™.

3. Draw a tree, using a large branch as a "unit" of measure. This, as with all measured drawings, can be matched against a traced drawing or photograph. In the studio space, measure larger parts of the room by utilizing chairs, drawing benches, etc., as units of measure.

4. Set up several objects at differing heights and distances apart. Check their relative positions to one another using A (angle) and S (size) measuring techniques.

5. Confirm and draw freehand different foreshortened views of objects using photographs (including the human body). By using tracing paper and contour lines, compare your freehand attempts to the traced version. What area would you use as 'home base'?

6. Draw room interiors, exterior architectural settings, and still-life arrangements to practice the A.S.P. measuring technique. Always sketch freely before applying exact measuring analysis.

7. Utilizing each of the rendering techniques described above, draw from the same still-life setup with one or two light sources. Note how each technique gives a different feel to the objects and the total scene.

8. Using a high-contrast, black-and-white photograph of a face, try hatching in one direction only, and then do a second drawing using multidirectional hatching.

9. Draw a still-life arrangement with extreme value scale, and then try the same scene with a scale much narrower in breadth (i.e., having the values closer to each other on the value scale). Observe how the stronger, more comprehensive scale gives a different, more solid feel than the narrow range.

10. Draw ellipses and arcs using just your fingers. Then draw the same objects using your wrist and arm. Note the improvement in these shapes and lines. Practice a figure eight at different scales.

11. On a sheet of sketch paper, practice changing the pressure with your hand in corner-to-corner, thick and thin lines, covering the entire sheet. Although easily understood, this, like the previous exercise is an eye/muscle technique requiring much actual physical practice.

12. Try blocking in shapes from a still-life setup using a combination of preliminary, straight layout lines and more organic, curving lines. Pay attention to how a change of weight (darkness) or thickness gives the illusion of depth. Use a B, 2B, and 4B pencil for different drawings to see how they vary in descriptive ability.

13. Using a stick of vine charcoal (soft grade), sketch freely from life at a park, zoo, or mall setting. Get used to its ability to produce strong, varied line suitable for figures and animals.

in review

1. What is the definition of the drawing rule "big before small; simple before complex"?

2. What three, minimum values are necessary to describe a drawn object as being dimensional?

3. What are the definitions of proportion and proportional measuring?

4. What are three techniques for rendering value in a drawing?

5. What does the acronym A.S.P. stand for?

solid drawing

objectives

Develop an understanding of the basic technical reasons for gesture drawing and how to apply gesture techniques to figure/observational drawing

Acquire an understanding of how gesture drawing is the foundation for and is applicable to longer studies

Gather knowledge about contour (line) drawing and how to apply contour drawing to general observational drawing and figure studies

Learn how contour drawing integrates with tonal studies

Learn how gesture drawing relates to sequence drawings

introduction

Understanding the nature of the *gesture drawing*, or quick sketch, is paramount to the animation artist. By its very name (gesture/quick sketch/scribble drawing), we can see that what is intended is *a kind of shorthand visual notation of an object, either in action or at rest.* Not only is the drawing giving us a simple idea of what the object looks like, but it is also showing us the nature or sense of *what* it is doing. When we say the "what" in that last sentence, we are talking about whether the thing being drawn is at rest or in motion, and the quality of that state of being. Being at rest can be a feather laying on a pillow, or a seventy-ton Brachiosaurus standing (or sinking!) on a sand bar. Motion can refer to a snail crawling slowly across a garden or a hawk in a 100-mph dive. A gesture contains within it something called the *line of action* (which can be quite static). *A line of action (or motion) is really a kind of imaginary axis (a line aligned with the length or width of a form) that moves along the direction of the action and major form(s) of the object in question.*

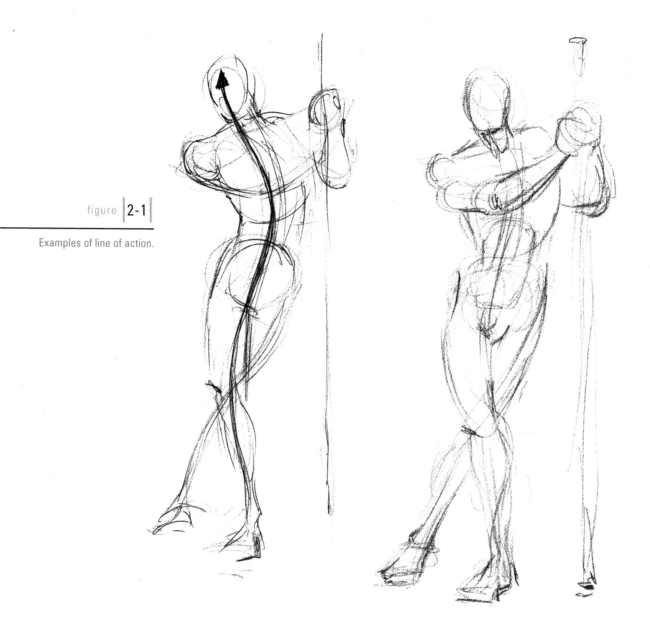

figure |2-1|

Examples of line of action.

LINES, LANDMARKS, AND SCRIBBLING

We can see that this line is only an abstract thought, not necessarily part of any specific contour or edge. This is a difficult concept for some beginning artists to grasp, largely due to the habit of learning to draw "things" by simply outlining them, rather than by understanding their internal dynamics. Internal dynamics can refer to many things: line of action, "landmark" signals (referring to skeletal or other substructure), muscular tension, costume or surface distortion, and so forth. Line is used to describe any of those as a kind of shorthand notation: several heavy lines might indicate a sense of mass, tension, or both in a preliminary character design.

figure |2-2|

Examples of different gesture sketches.

| NOTE |

Landmarks?

No, we don't mean the Washington Monument or Mt. Rushmore. In this case, landmarks refer to anatomical elements of the figure that help us to correctly place other body parts and/or their positions in space. For instance, the breastbone and the belly button provide clues as to where the vertical midline of the torso lies. The positions of the clavicle and the iliac crests provide information on the inclination of the shoulders and hips.

| NOTE |

As Moves the Spine,
so Does the Line

Typically, the line of action follows the movement of the spine. Since the torso is the largest flexible element of the human figure, its torsion/position is key in suggesting movement.

More experienced artists have all this in mind even when drawing just a simple contour sketch. Much of this is implied in how the lines are handled; their quality and placement infer much information. Gesture drawings can therefore give cues to the viewer about aspects of the object(s) that may not be seen directly.

A gesture or quick sketch has the look of an almost casual or loose, rhythmic multiple-line version of something.

| NOTE |

Scribbling, Technically Speaking…

Heavy scribbling with a dark medium can result in an unreadable drawing. The answer: *draw with a light touch using a tool that creates minimal value and then refine the drawing with a darker medium.* Also, beware of using charcoal over graphite! Graphite is not only a drawing medium but is also used as a lubricant. Charcoal tends to skip over the lines of a preliminary drawing. Also, charcoal is matte and graphite is shiny. This may lead to unwanted visual "pop," where the pencil shows through the charcoal and causes broken lines.

These extra lines often denote energy, direction, weight, or implied complexity. The loose scribbles of the pencil quickly build the idea of volume in the drawing. The extra lines show problem solving: trying to find volume and shape. Without these lines, the drawing actually does not contain enough information. Beginning artists often are disturbed at the seeming lack of "photorealism" that these drawings display. What they don't realize is that a poor initial understanding of an object and its state can rob the final drawing of all its life and interest. As we explain to our life-drawing classes, it's okay to have extra lines. Each scribble should be a part of the system and be thoughtfully placed. *Don't scribble for the sake of scribbling; scribble to build volume.* After a while, life-drawing students will realize that from such "simple" beginnings, very polished and refined drawings can result. An extra benefit from doing a few gesture drawings is that the artist can warm up, much in the same way an athlete warms up before a contest.

In a way, we are visual athletes. It takes endurance, focus, and a kind of mental strength to be a top-flight artist. Intense and prolonged efforts along with innate ability are necessary to produce an artist, not merely talent.

figure |2-3|

Skeletal similarities shared by humans and animals.

figure | 2-4 |

Skeletal gesture drawings.

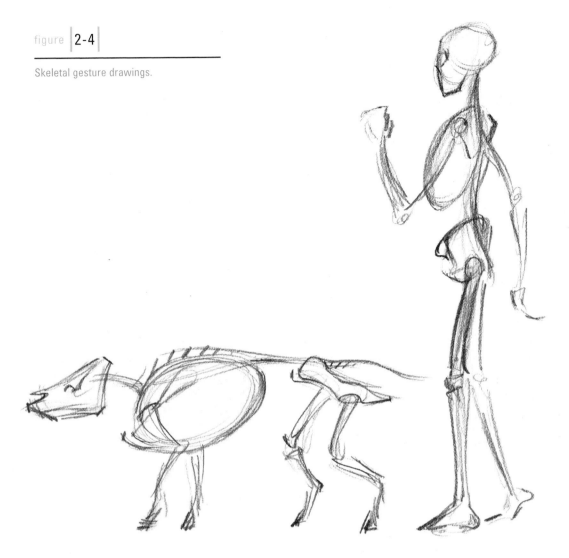

IT'S ALIVE!!!

"Living things" is a very broad term. As an artist and animator, you may be called upon to draw trees, dinosaurs, bacteria, aliens, or nineteenth-century English villains. The range is so broad that, as an artist, you must have some common way of dealing with such disparate living things. Generally, we group things to draw by common structural traits. This means that you would practice drawing people, lions, and stegosaurs in a like fashion because they all share similar skeletal structures, muscular systems, and movement modes.

Small changes in even these systems will have major impacts on how things run, slither, walk, fly, or otherwise engage in locomotion. Simplifying these creatures into shapes and lines becomes easier once you understand that an oval for a rib cage, a line for the spine, and a saddle or similar shape for the pelvis will give you the framework from which to make two- and four-legged beasts.

The main thrust of movement is normally generated along the spine or at least parallel to it (that pesky line of action, again), because the spine aligns itself along the length of a creature, and so is naturally going the direction of the line of action. Despite differences in shoulder girdle and pelvis, movement by and large will still take the same general path for these living beings. Differences in locomotion occur by size, limb proportion, type of pelvic attachment to limbs, flexibility of the spine, and so on. For example, the long, extremely flexible spine of a cheetah allows it to literally whip its body up and down as it runs to achieve the most extreme leg extension and thus greatest speed, while a mastodon's columnar legs remain comparatively stiff so as to support the animal's massive weight as it walks.

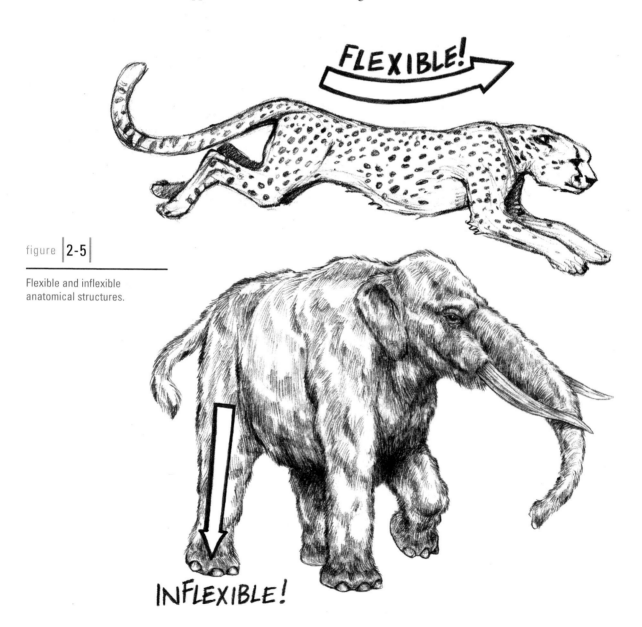

figure | 2-5 |

Flexible and inflexible anatomical structures.

figure | 2-6 |

Similarities of line
in gesture drawings.

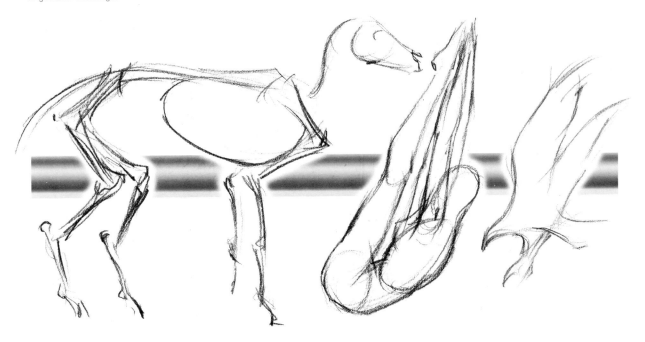

After drawing from a live model, you will notice that drawing, say, a lion, is no longer quite the foreign, abstract puzzle it once was. All of the simple, drawn forms that work for the human body also work for lions, albeit in a slightly altered form. Due to this factor, swift analysis of other creatures and movement is possible from just an initial study of the human form. The large, simple hand movements that we use to describe a woman diving can also be used for a hawk in flight because of the considerable "biomorphic" (living shape) overlap from birds to people to dogs to sheep.

We touched upon this topic in Chapter 1, and we wish only to add that as a hand/eye coordination skill, drawing does take some time to accomplish. It is definitely a hands-on situation.

Some living things, however, require a bit of study. For example, a sea turtle in motion does not obey the same dictates that a human swimmer does, because the shell of the turtle is attached to the spine, rendering it inflexible.

INFLEXIBLE!

figure | 2-7 |

Inflexible action in a sea turtle.

The flippers seem to move independently of the body. This situation becomes more extreme when one looks at something like a squid or jellyfish, where structural similarities to us are dim at best. But, the curvilinear forms and fluidity of motion can still be described fairly easily by natural hand and arm motions, even in this drawing situation.

A living creature normally has some type of curvature to its body and often in its motion, and organic motion follows this curve. This lends itself to the rules of animation that govern the natural arc of motion and drawing techniques in quick sketching.

figure | 2-8 |

Jellyfish drawn with natural "curvilinear" motions of the hand.

Sequential drawing, or stop-action drawing, is really a series of gestures or quick sketches that show the different steps of an action in chronological order. Think of stop-action photography. It can be quickly seen that this is the first step toward actual animating, whether by hand or on a computer. The analysis of movement allows the animator/artist to provide a blueprint for a complete activity. By concentrating on the essential information (line of action, quality of action, and simple proportions of things in motion), a lively and exciting animation can result. This is a natural outgrowth of quick sketching. To dwell on details or perfect outlines actually reduces the naturalness of the object and its motion. All information of this kind can be added in later steps of the animation process.

Always remember that drawing is problem solving. The artist that draws from life is putting down a series of marks on a piece of paper (or other surface), in an attempt to visually approximate the subject of the drawing, and to make the viewers believe that they perceive a replication of a dimensional object in the drawing. This is accomplished through good drawing skills and representation clues (like value and perspective).

STILL LIFE

Quick sketches can also describe inanimate objects. Most of us are familiar with fast architectural drawings done on site, or sketches of race cars, wagons drawn by horses, rock formations, and so on.

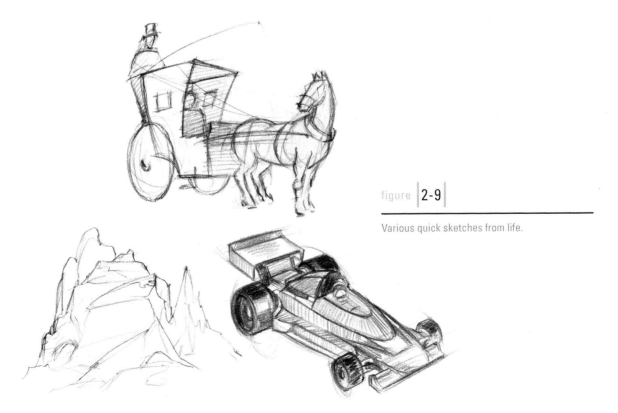

figure 2-9

Various quick sketches from life.

Despite the fact that in many of these cases there will be no line of action, and perhaps no action at all, the artist can still give valuable information about a scene or object by using quick sketching techniques. As in drawing living things, quick sketching of inanimate objects or settings reduces information to a useable size and gives a first, gut reaction to the qualities most important for other artists.

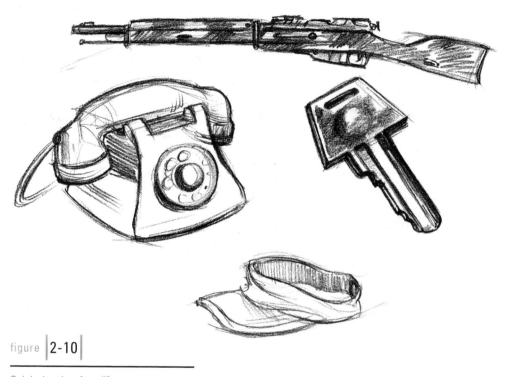

figure | 2-10 |

Quick sketches from life.

Of first importance is finding out what information is essential in describing something. We don't need to know the surface texture of a tree bark before knowing the overall structure of the trunk and limbs. Many artists discover that they are happier and more suited to drawing scenic or textural subjects than in character design. This may lead to a career in background art or texture mapping or other extensions of drawing.

LINE, HOOK, AND SINKER

The weight of a line, or its sharpness, fuzziness, or repetition all give visual clues to the viewer that the form being described is not flat. In quick sketches, a change in line thickness (weight) is a natural outcome of hand and arm movement, and immediately breathes more life into the drawing.

Heavy line can indicate mass or weight, or spatial distance from the viewers. This happens because the brain assumes by association that a heavier line resembles something either heavier, partly shaded, or closer to the viewer. Multiple lines give a sense of motion, defocusing, or general modeling, and can also constitute refinement of form as the artist reworks and defines an area.

figure **2-11**

Line variation in gesture drawings.

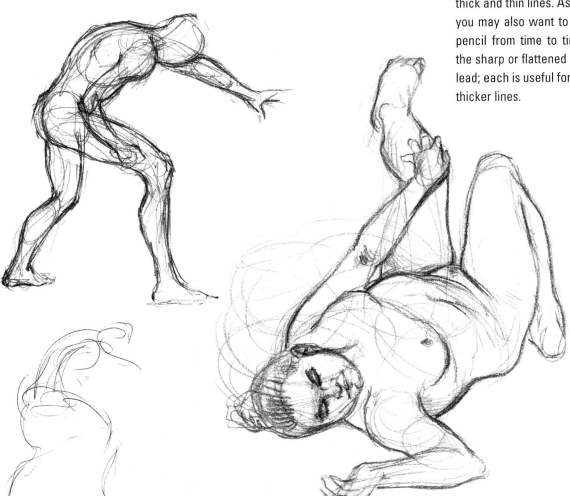

| **NOTE** |

Returning to the theme of drawing as a physical activity, we must include the control of *pressure* on the drawing tool, whether it is a pencil, pen, or any other medium. By using the correct grip and hand position, it should be relatively easy for you to change the pressure "up and down" to alternately produce thick and thin lines. As you draw, you may also want to rotate the pencil from time to time to find the sharp or flattened part of the lead; each is useful for thinner or thicker lines.

By losing the line occasionally or giving it some softness or fuzziness, we can also change the sense of distance, or give the illusion of depth of field, or even that an object, by focused and unfocused lines, has depth.

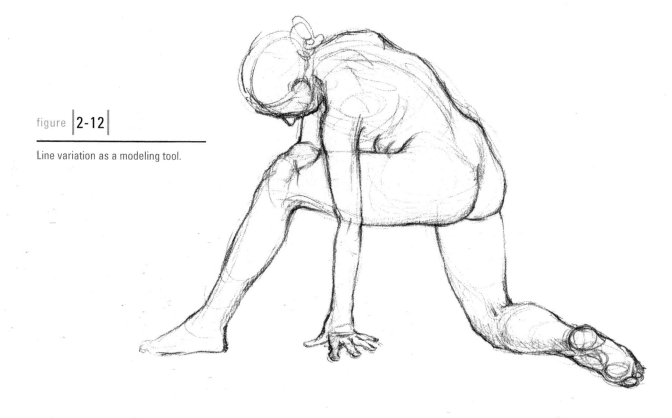

figure |2-12|

Line variation as a modeling tool.

Examples shown here are far more descriptive than words. You are encouraged to also look at the old master and contemporary master drawings.

From Gesture to Finish Line

Remember: a gesture drawing is a quick sketch designed to capture the visual movement and pose of the figure (important in character animation!), not specific detail or character. It is the framework upon which we can then build a more refined drawing.

What are the ways and means of moving from a gesture drawing to a more finished piece? A logical progression is to move from the general action/motion-oriented quick sketch to a partial contour/partial simple structure drawing. *That is, by eliminating excess line with the eraser and adding some actual contours (like the quadriceps muscle group on the leg), and then*

figure 2-13

Gesture sketches with various line modifications.

adding a stronger rib and pelvis form under the muscles, an intermediate drawing emerges that still contains the life of the original gesture sketch, but now has more specific information about the object (in this case, a person).

As the gesture drawing is a loose compilation of fast, observational line, the next stage of development is a reduction in the amount of "wandering" line, where we begin to emphasize the direction of action (if applicable, as in a more open pose), and to clarify bony and muscular structures. So in this stage—the most crucial in a drawing—the major structures (in this case human) become more significant linear observations, that is, closer to anatomical reality: the strong lines defined by the thigh (front and back), lower leg (bony front and flexor back), massive rib cage, collar bones and shoulder muscles, back (spine and aligned muscles), and pelvis (with bony upper front and muscle/fat lower bottom), along with the arms (bony and muscular forearms, biceps, and triceps on upper arm) and neck. Although somewhat darker perhaps (be careful not to darken too much!), these structural drawings are not yet at a final stage of refinement.

figure |2-14|

Transforming a gesture drawing into a partly finished contour drawing.

This addition and simplification of line can be done to any quick sketch, depending upon what is essential to the object(s) being drawn. We are reducing the extra linear information that we initially used to find the pose and some basic shapes and linear action. As in any structure, what is significant in scale and structural integrity is what we concentrate on, without losing the importance of the pose. Remember, even a house key or an automobile has a "pose." All things have a certain directional emphasis, or at least a stationary sense to them. As you record each item, look for what is important to its overall structure and character.

We pointed out what was essential to include in the human structure as you develop it; look for the same kind of information when defining other living things or even inanimate objects (both small and large). An example could be a Ferrari; it has certain large parts (hood and tires), some smaller, ancillary elements (mirrors, lug nuts), and also a definite line of action (which is permanent in this case). *A gesture would define the action and large elements somewhat loosely, and a second stage, contour drawing would tighten these observations into a clearer picture of the body, engine area, tires, hood, and so forth.*

So a racecar, a water buffalo, a bridge, or an Olympic sprinter can all be further developed in this way. The physical motions involved in such drawing are initiated from the arm and wrist, rather than from smaller finger motions. This produces a set of natural curves and straight lines of the size and energy necessary for complete, dynamic drawings that are applicable especially to animation. As we have emphasized, drawings that are too small or picky in detail lack the look and overall accuracy that animation, even computer driven, needs.

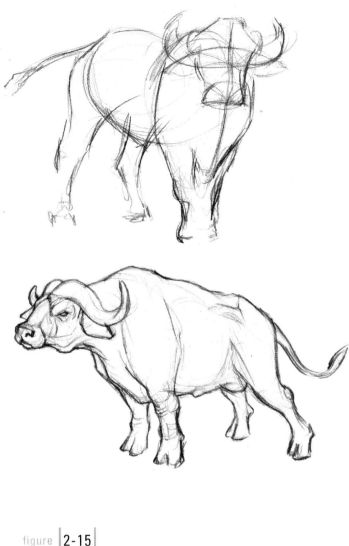

figure **2-15**

Stages of linear development for a water buffalo.

It's Alive (or not)!!!

To draw inanimate objects, you may want to use photographs or diagrams for reference. These could reveal subtle (or not so subtle) structures that will influence how to approach the final rendering. For animate subjects such as people or animals, anatomical study becomes a primary tool, along with life studies, and photographic and film references. *In all cases, larger forms and simple renderings still are the first step in recording and developing each subject.* It becomes more obvious now why this is necessary: details do not tell us anything about the overall action, structure, or feel of an object. Accumulating details will usually overwhelm what the artist is trying to say about a subject. For example, the fur of a wolf, although important, does not describe the action of a leap, the emotion of snarling canine fury, or many other appearances or attributes of the wolf.

Looking at a variety of sketches in progress will give you some idea of how a preliminary drawing gets developed.

figure | 2-16 |

Stages of drawing development.

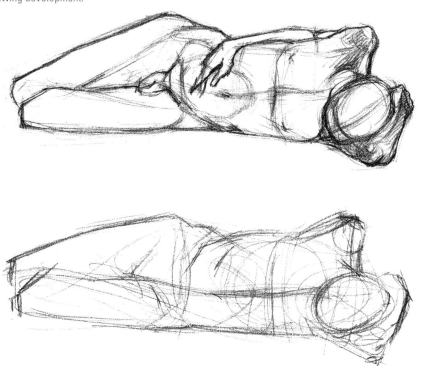

In this section, we've noted how the final forms were often already implied in the gesture sketch, and parts of the musculature and/or skeleton were a basis for some of the gesture. Similar observations can be made in drawings that are not based on the human body.

GESTURES AND PEOPLE:
MORE THAN JUST HAND MOVEMENTS

The human figure is actually just one special case of gesture drawings. The term gesture already cues us to think of people; people make gestures. However, the entire figure can be thought of as having a "gesture." It can have an attitude, or display a myriad assortment of poses and positions, as in dance or athletics. We touched on this in Chapter 1. It now becomes obvious that learning anatomy and the mechanics of motion are absolutely essential in order to understand what we see and to represent it on paper. To draw a gesture, remember that it is the action (remember the *line of action?*) that is of primary importance. You do *not* have to start with the head. Frankly, the spine, shoulders, and torso have more to say about a pose than the head. It is just psychological habit to think of the head (and therefore the face) as the first and most important thing to draw.

The following are examples of various gesture drawings in different stages of development. Some figures are short and stout, others very athletic. In each case, the most important information has a common set of visual and proportional elements, although emphasized in different ways because of the innate differences in the figures.

figure | 2-17

Some different figurative sketches.

Now, here are a couple examples of beginning to end gesture drawings. As part of your exercises, you might copy these and then apply this to your own work.

figure |2-18|

Gesture drawings in development.

And here are some examples of drawings where the skeletal factor is emphasized to demonstrate how this applies to actual posed drawing situations.

figure | 2-19 |

Gestures utilizing the simplified skeleton.

Further development of inanimate objects with contour line can be somewhat confusing when only described in words, so a couple examples of this stage of finish in this class of drawing subjects are shown in the next figure.

figures | 2-20 |

Studies from life; contour development
of inanimate objects.

ALL IS NOT LOST: CONTOUR DRAWING IS HERE!

Now we will return to the evolution of the quick sketch into a more finished line drawing. A contour drawing is a line drawing. What this means is that we are producing a replica of something by the use of line only. This immediately proposes a set of questions. For example, what exactly is a useful line in a contour drawing? Although we might take for granted the types of lines used in cartoons and animation, after a bit of looking, we can discover why these particular lines were chosen.

Looking back several thousand years, one can see that descriptions of animals and humans had already gotten quite sophisticated as judged by the prehistoric cave paintings found in France, Spain, and North Africa. It is interesting to note that even at this early date, an outline had been used to describe much of the subject. When we say outline, we are actually referring to two separate but similar things. *One is the silhouette of the object; that is, its shape where the object ends and its visual surroundings begin for any viewer.* This refers to a flat, specifically defined shape that can be described by tracing it on any transparent surface between the eye and the object. The shape is what we see transferred to this imaginary pane of glass, and it can be translated into a line. So immediately it becomes apparent that the line is pure fiction, more like the

THE ANIMATOR AT WORK

Winsor McCay

One of the earliest animators was Canadian born Winsor McCay (1867–1934). Known for his animation shorts *Little Nemo* and *Gertie the Dinosaur,* McCay actually started as a portrait artist and caricaturist in what were then called "dime museums," entertainment venues with carnival acts, "freak shows," and vaudevillian productions. He was also attending a business college at the behest of his father. But with a true interest in art, McCay left school, and at the age of twenty-one, began doing posters for the National Printing Company of Chicago, followed by a stint in

Cincinnati creating illustrated posters for the Kohl and Middleton Dime Museum. All of this experience culminated in a technique that was by necessity both entertaining and fast. Billboards were becoming more prevalent by this time, and McCay worked in that arena as well. His reputation began to grow, as his work became more nationally known.

Marrying in 1891, McCay soon had two children and a wife to support, and he found it necessary to join the *Cincinnati Commercial Tribune* newspaper as a cartoonist/reporter in order to pay his bills. With the short deadlines and numerous mini-jobs inherent in the newspaper business, McCay's technique became even more refined and extremely quick. This would be a great asset to him later in his exploration of animation. In addition to his nominal job with the newspaper, McCay did freelance illustration work for various other publications. 1902 proved to be a pivotal year for the artist; he had started a cartoon strip called *Tales of the Jungle Imps by Felix Fiddle,* which began his interest in sequential art, a precursor to animation. Later that year, the *New York Herald* newspaper contacted him and asked him to work for them; he moved with his wife and children to New York to begin this new adventure. Within this context, he began further experimentation with cartoon strips, which were then becoming vogue among the public.

During this time he developed two very successful cartoon strips, *Dream of a Rarebit Fiend* and *Little Sammy Sneeze,* both appearing in 1904. Because of contractual conflicts between the two newspapers that he worked for, McCay used the alias "Silas" for one of the strips. The following year he started a new strip called *Little Nemo in Slumberland,* where fantasy and youthful adventures were mixed in a masterful blend. His draftsmanship was fluid and incredibly facile, allowing him to construct his stories in remarkably short time. Interestingly enough, *Little Nemo in Slumberland* was made into a Broadway musical at that time. In fact, McCay had begun his own vaudeville act, where he drew on an act called *Speed Drawing,* creating his own characters in short order for the audience. He continued doing strips for various papers and editorial cartoons, as well.

After moving from the *Herald* to William Randolph Hearst's *The New York American* newspaper and always restless for something new, McCay began toying with the idea of producing actual filmed strips, animated shorts utilizing his rapid drawing technique. Using characters from *Little Nemo,* McCay succeeded in producing his first (and wildly successful) animations. He worked out the timing and camera techniques through trial and error, and did all of his own drawing, a most amazing feat when the volume of drawing is considered. Next came his animation *How the Mosquito Operates,* which followed the first animation in gaining great popularity among audiences.

Hearst felt that these adventures were taking away from time at the paper, and McCay was finally forbidden to even do cartoon strips, limiting him to only editorial cartoons. Vaudeville, as well, was banned from McCay's repertoire of activity. Perhaps as a response to this, McCay continued his experiments with animation, producing several more animated films, including the famous 1918 *Sinking of the Lusitania.* Remaining as an editorial cartoonist, Winsor McCay died in 1934 of a stroke. His legacy to animation was original and important.

figure 2-21

Tone emphasized over line.

border on a map that cannot actually be seen from an airplane. The line is where the object ends, pure and simple. And when tone is added to the line (outline), the emphasis shifts from the line to the tone as the primary tool for description.

The second meaning of outline is any line following the apparent edge of a form where that form is distinct from other forms either underneath or adjacent to it. This means that not only a silhouette shape but also any internal shapes can be described by line.

figure 2-22

Contour line and the figure;
external and internal structure described.

The combination of the two provides us with a contour drawing. A subset of this second definition of outline is any line that describes a change of plane or significant structural change, such as a cheekbone or wrinkle. *Where there is a significant change of planar direction (that is, where flat surfaces bend toward another direction), a line can be placed (if the change is sharp enough).*

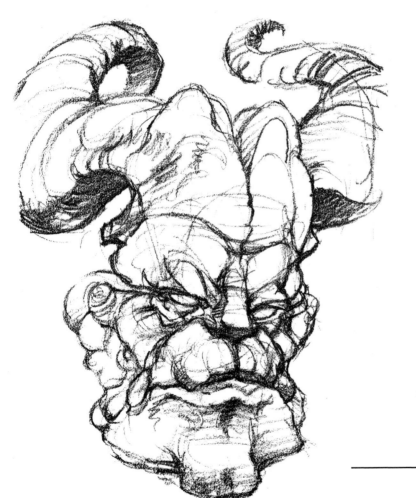

figure |2-23|

Structural contour lines
in a character design.

Why use an outline at all? The most evident reasons are for *speed* and *flexibility.* We have already seen this in gesture drawings. Although tonal gestures are possible, it is line that is the master of this genre because of its sheer practicality. Animation grew from this speed and simplicity. It is hard to imagine how any other technique could have engineered the development of two-dimensional animation. The trick is to utilize outline in such a way as to imply more interior structure than is actually drawn. This involves a careful analysis of what gives those clues, and trying out many preliminary drawings until the "feel" is just right. This is another reason why we emphasize the importance of drawing many, many preliminary sketches.

DRAWING FROM <u>BOTH</u> SIDES OF THE BRAIN!

It would appear that human beings are hard-wired to use the contour line as their predominant or "fallback" method of delineating 2D forms. This leads to the unfortunate phenomenon of "switching gears," which often takes place during life-drawing sessions. When working on a quick sketch, we draw rapidly to describe various volumes and masses, working from simple forms toward more complex forms. Unfortunately, when the drawing begins to take longer to finish (ten or more minutes in duration), a mental switch is thrown in our heads and we revert to our base drawing methods, which manifest themselves in a tight pencil grip and the need to describe the figure in methodical contours and meticulous detail. We must always start out with a gesture drawing for any figure study. Remember, it is at this stage that we begin to correct anatomy and proportion to help ensure a successful drawing. Using contour line in a drawing is our most basic drawing convention. Even children use this method to translate their vision of the world into drawings.

MAGIC ACT: GESTURE TO CONTOUR

The development of contour from gesture is mostly a matter of massed line and direction being reduced to a simple outline. This can be seen in the following examples, where an implied figure becomes a more defined one. In this case, a loose, surface gestural tone has been applied, as well, to further enhance the forms.

After producing the quick sketch in this way, several directions in which to proceed are presented to the artist. Line can become an end in itself or a precursor to tonality.

figure 2-24

Gestural sketch in development with tonal elements.

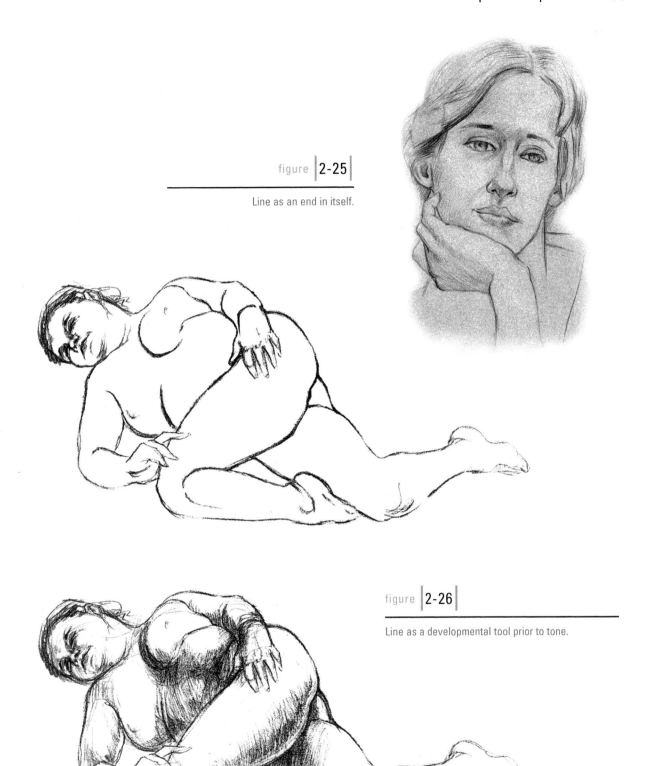

figure |2-25|

Line as an end in itself.

figure |2-26|

Line as a developmental tool prior to tone.

figure **2-27**

figure **2-27**

Clean animation line.

Some line is, quite frankly, more "artsy," with fuzzy, loose portions, thick and thin sections, and other transformations. Line for animation is cleaner, defined, more to the point.

Knowledge of proportion and anatomy are very important. As a drawing develops, this previous knowledge of images of musculature and bone speeds up the process by "shortcutting" through observation. The trap here is when we completely substitute what we think we should be drawing for what we are actually seeing. Later, drawing from our own imagination is useful— even required—but only as the result of much preliminary study.

figure **2-28**

Always begin with a gesture!

| NOTE |

Step Away from the Chalk...

We must remember to always start with the gesture drawing, and not attempt to do pure outline as our quick sketch. Otherwise, we may end up with an extremely flat shape that looks more like a police chalk outline than it does a figure.

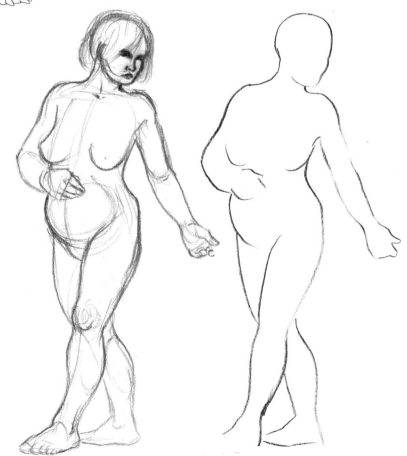

A contour drawing can be either fluid and full of life, or stiff and deadly. What makes the difference? Starting with a good gesture drawing will lead to an excellent contour drawing. Shared characteristics are the key. *By confining the contours to real anatomy, significant structure, and well-observed proportion, a line drawing can come to life if the artist avoids excessive generic observation.* Too much reduction of the line to oversimplified forms and the subject begins to become static. A similar error on the side of extra curvy and bulging form gives a kind of hallucinatory, wiggly monstrosity. Some less successful superhero and monster characters are victims of this latter problem. This does not mean that complex forms and wild dimensions cannot succeed. Just proceed with a little common sense, as when adding seasoning to food: some can be great, but too much can cause problems.

Some examples of successful contour drawings are shown in the following figure.

In these drawings, you will note that an economy of techniques, good observation, and controlled line quality are keys to success. Contour line should be used carefully and thoughtfully to refine the volume and details of the figure.

figure | 2-29 |

Successful contour drawings with some tone.

The Living Contour

Life drawing is the primary tool for achieving technical excellence in line drawing. If you can draw the human body, you can draw anything. The figure is both complex and repetitive, containing similar curves and forms, yet with subtle variances and planar changes that make all the difference. Taking classes with a technically grounded instructor is generally the best path to choose. Even practice at drawing a model without an instructor can be valuable. The key is to learn to be aware of what you are really looking at, and to consciously apply the proportional, physical, and anatomical techniques to all of your drawing. It is a good idea to confine your drawings to timed intervals. *Since much of animation is founded on quick sketching, devel-*

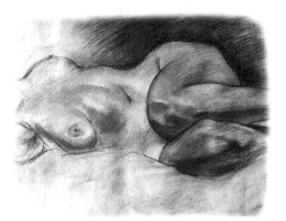

oping this skill is a primary goal. Try to do a minimum of ten gestures of a minute or less in duration, followed by successively longer poses, lasting up to thirty minutes long. A pose lasting longer than thirty minutes becomes a long study, and although valuable, is not something you need to dwell on in the beginning. Some examples of timed figure drawings follow in the next figure.

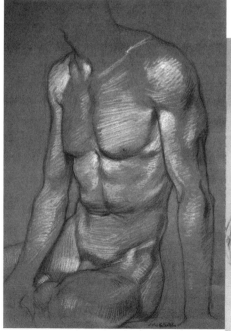

figure | 2-30 |

Longer finished figure studies.

OKAY, NOW DO A LONG DRAWING

Contour drawings can be developed into completely rendered light and dark studies, even color studies. This final type of product is used to show character development, lighting, color, and texture mapping skills for the 2D artist in a 3D animation environment. A longer session, which is broken into twenty- or thirty-minute sittings by the model, is the core of the exercise. A setup of two or more good light sources can give enough shadowing to the figure to make an interesting drawing. As mentioned in Chapter 1, a minimum of three values, carefully chosen to provide enough contrast, is required to turn the line drawing into something that appears real. The lines can remain as part of the final product . . . or disappear altogether as tone takes over entirely.

figure |2-31|

Integration of line and tone.

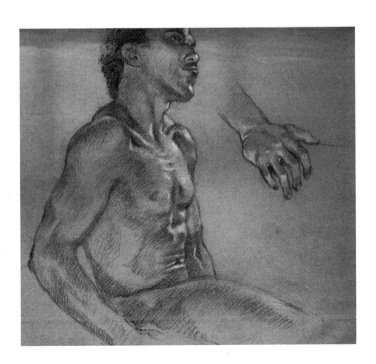

figure |2-32|

Tonal emphasis in a longer figure study.

Gradation is the most applicable technique here, although hatching is valuable as well. Color studies in water-based, oil-based, or other mediums can follow eventually. All of these may prove valuable to the artist as a designer, character developer, background artist, etc. Some of these are shown below, and some appear in the color section of this book.

It is important to observe where shadows have sharp edges and where the edges feather to light or other darker areas. Reflected light helps carve out the form, but should not become overpowering. The overall light and dark scale should be fairly broad, which helps the viewer to recognize the form. Surface detail should enhance the overall sculptural quality of the form, but should not get in the way of three-dimensionality. Drawings that are partly rendered, as opposed to being more simply developed overall, can be highly successful if there is enough information for the eye.

figure | 2-33 |

Figure studies in several rendering techniques.

figure | 2-34 |

Partly rendered figure study.

These can be of value to the designer and director, because they still have much of the original action in them due to their line quality. Full-color renderings done in marker, gouache, watercolor, or oil may require separate classes that concentrate on each type of material. These additional techniques can help to round out an artist's skill set and also add to marketability.

CHAPTER SUMMARY

The use of line to suggest mass, motion, and perspective in living things and inanimate objects is important to drawing for animation. The quick sketch is an integral starting point for building refined line drawings that become the basis for effective character and environment construction through contour line use. The functionality of gesture drawing as it applies to the human figure is directly affected by observation of life and a working knowledge of anatomy. Mastering the quick sketch and the contour drawing are crucial to the animator's skill set.

exercises

1. Using a live model for a twenty- to thirty-minute session, practice gesture drawings, each one taking only thirty seconds to two minutes to draw.

2. Drawing from live or photographic resources, describe humans in a variety of poses using only skeletal hints and cues.

3. Drawing from live reference in an actual situation such as a mall, zoo, or school setting, record what you see in short, thirty-second to two-minute observations.

4. Draw quick sketches of inanimate objects. Try drawing objects of various sizes with the idea in mind of representing their structural essence.

5. Draw architectural settings with the same quick sketch technique. Keep your observations to a few minutes at a time to prevent getting obsessed with detail.

6. Take some of your sketches and develop them into partly finished contour drawings. Look at the examples in this chapter as a guide or study such artists as Tintoretto or Daumier.

7. Draw from a live human figure two or three times weekly.

8. Practice drawing two-minute, five-minute, ten-minute, and fifteen-minute studies, each time following a warm-up period of gesture drawings. Then, cycle the session times back the other way: fifteen-minute, ten-minute, five-minute, two-minute, and more one-minute drawings.

9. Practice sequence drawings for fifteen to thirty minutes at a time. Some sequences can be complete, and some can have steps missing that need to be filled in. Three-, four-, or five-step sequences are best for learning this technique.

10. Draw the human figure for thirty minutes to four hours in a single pose, concentrating on proportion, anatomy, lighting, and overall impact.

11. Draw the figure as a gesture sketch, then develop it as a contour sketch, and then finally finish it as a tonal study (in separate sessions).

12. Draw the figure in sections only, concentrating on the hands, feet, head, and so on; do some as line drawings and some as tonal studies.

13. Take a drawn figure and translate it into color, using markers (on board or marker paper), watercolor, acrylic, or other media.

14. Using a developed fifteen- to twenty-minute value drawing, retrace it in contour and redevelop it as a new value study. Try hatching and crosshatching in the new study.

in review

1. What is a *gesture drawing*?

2. What is meant by the term *landmarks* in reference to observational drawing?

3. What is the definition of *line of action*?

4. What are two meanings for *outline* or *contour* as they refer to drawing?

THE ART OF CREATIVITY

robin landa

Robin Landa is an accomplished author of books on art and design. A professor at Kean University, Robin gives lectures around the country and has been interviewed extensively on the subjects of design, creativity, and art. She also serves as a creative consultant to major corporations.

Creativity seems mysterious. When I ask illustrious creative directors, art directors, designers, and copywriters how they come up with creative ideas, many claim that they don't know. Some say they don't think about a problem directly, but, rather, go off to take in a film or museum exhibit and a solution seems to come to them in a state of relaxation. Other creatives are able to articulate something about their thinking process:

"I noticed how…"

"I saw that and thought of this."

"I heard someone say…"

"I thought, What if…"

After years of doing research into creative thinking—observing, teaching, designing, writing, formulating theories, and interviewing hundreds of creative professionals—I noted some fascinating commonalties among creative thinkers. What seems to distinguish a creative mind may seem, at first, unremarkable; however, upon further examination, one can see why the following markers can yield rich creative output.

BEING SHARP-EYED Part of almost any design or art education is learning to be an active viewer/seer. Whether you learn to draw a blind contour or observe the position of forms in space, you learn to be completely attentive to the visual world. Maintaining that state of alertness, of being a sharp-eyed observer, allows one to notice the inherent creative possibilities in any given situation. Being watchful when observing one's surroundings, everyday juxtapositions, allows one to see what others may miss or not even think is of note.

BEING RECEPTIVE If you've ever worked with or lived with a stubborn person, then you know the value of a person who is flexible, open to suggestions, other opinions, constructive criticism, and different schools of thought. Receptivity, as a marker of creativity, means more than being open to ideas. It means embracing the notion of incoming information, and new ideas.

Being flexible allows one to let go of dogmatic thinking, and to shift when necessary, to bend with the path of a blossoming idea.

COURAGE Having the courage to take risks is part of the creative spirit.

For many, the fear of failure or appearing foolish inhibits risk-taking. Fear squashes that inner voice urging you to go out on a creative limb. Fearlessness coupled with intellectual curiosity, a desire to explore and be an adventurer, an interest in many things (not just one thing), rather than play it safe and comfortable, feeds creativity.

ASSOCIATIVE THINKING The ability to connect the outwardly unconnected feeds creative thinking. Bring two old things together to form a new combination. Merge two objects into a seamless different one. Creative people seem to be able to arrange associative hierarchies in ways that allow them to make connections that might seem remote to, or even, elude all others.

Creativity is truly a way of thinking, a way of examining the world and interacting with information and ideas. Whether you're designing a book jacket or taking a photograph doesn't matter. What matters is how you think about almost anything. When you are sharp-eyed, stay receptive, have courage, think associatively, and approach life with energy, then your work will be buoyed.

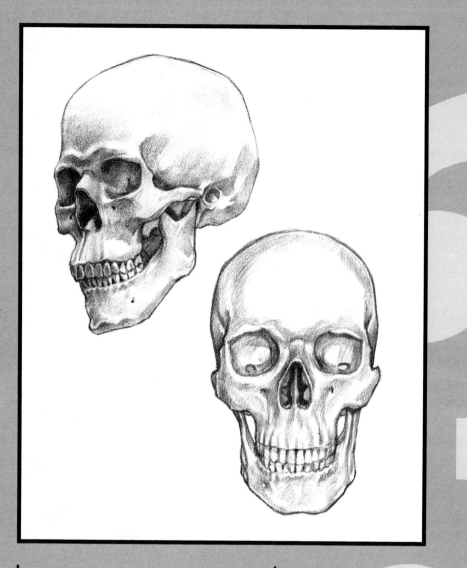

anatomy: human, inhuman, and critters

objectives

Learn about basic human anatomy

Gain a brief introduction to animal anatomy

Find out about drawing issues for animators relating to anatomy

Visualize life drawing as an essential skill for animators

Grasp the relationship of how anatomy relates to gesture drawing

Develop an understanding of the live model's role as reference for animators

introduction

Living things have insides and outsides. Most artists that draw, paint, sculpt, and create living creatures on computers have at least a rudimentary knowledge of the structure of animals and plants. In fact, there is a whole cottage industry of anatomy and posing books available to aid artists in drawing people, dogs, horses, and a host of other beings. As far as the vegetable kingdom goes, instruction books are more scarce, but some older "how-to" art books and publications dealing with botanical illustration have usable information about trees and plants that are used in art. Rather than being unnecessarily detailed about this subject, we will concentrate on those things that really do impact animation and solid drawing, in general. In this chapter, we hope to give a fresh outlook on how anatomy, movement, and animation are linked.

ANATOMY: HUMAN, INHUMAN, AND CRITTERS

THE HIPBONE'S CONNECTED TO THE THIGHBONE, THE THIGHBONE'S CONNECTED TO THE...

Before anything else is said, let's look at some basics in *human* anatomy. First, *everything hinges, literally, on the skeleton in vertebrate animals.* The skeleton determines where, how far, and how fast a living thing can move. Relative bone lengths along with muscle sizes and attachment determine the speed of vertebrate motion. Over time, a really long time, the skeleton developed from a simple, long whiplash sort of thing in primitive prefish, to the elaborate, multitasking core of a human being.

Animals all developed in different directions; we talk about it to demonstrate the versatility of this biomechanical tool, the skeleton. Obviously, unless you are going to become an orthopedic surgeon, complex explanation is unnecessary. However, total ignorance in this area can lead to some strange and unhappy solutions in animation. Happily, cartoon animation can bypass some of this information. But even there, a sound, basic anatomical knowledge is important (think the coyote-like appearance of Warner Brothers' Wile E. Coyote). More realistic animation and character design requires all motion to evolve out of the underlying skeletal structure. An example is that dragons, without exception, cannot really fly as portrayed in all fantasy art and animation. They would need an enormous wingspan and muscle overlaying a remarkable skeletal design made of some amazing bone/titanium alloy in order to just get off the ground.

Sometimes we indulge in denial when designing such things, but at some point a realistic run cycle for a six-legged buffalo would need some serious preliminary bone and muscle redesign. In looking at human anatomy, we will get a basic primer on most related animal anatomy as well, because of the commonality of most of the skeletal and musculature features.

| NOTE |

Square Cubes?

The "square-cube" rule, sometimes known as the "law of scaling," is a physical principle that shows that an increase in the size of an object (A=size) is not directly proportional to its relative increase in weight (B=weight). According to this rule, if an evil scientist enlarges a common lizard by a factor of 10 (hoping to create "The Beast That Ate Hoboken"), its width and depth would increase by 10, so A=10x10 or 100.

Unfortunately for our villain (and the lizard), the lizard's weight would increase by a factor based on width x depth x height: B=10x10x10 or 1,000.

The strength of bones and muscles is dependent on their cross-sectional area, which would not have scaled up enough for the lizard to be able to support himself. It's just not realistic.

ON TO THE HUMAN SKELETON!

Let's take a look at how the human skeleton is organized. Although not precisely as an anatomist would determine it, for the artist, *the skeleton is divided into two main parts: the axial and appendicular skeletons. The axial refers to the core or center; that is, head, spine, rib cage, and (although not anatomically quite accurate) the pelvis.*

figure | 3-1 |

The axial skeleton.

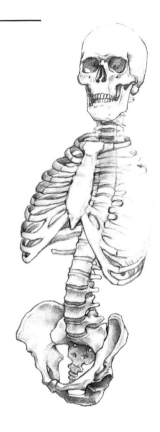

Basically, it's where things attach, where the origin of motion is, and where the center of gravity is determined. *The arms, legs, hands, feet, and shoulder girdle (scapula and clavicle) comprise the appendicular skeleton.*

The appendicular portion of the skeleton attaches to the axial portion, and is dependent upon it, although the legs and feet play an important role in all movement and posing. Occasionally bones provide some of the surface detail of the figure, such as in the head, knees, hands, and feet, and so on. *The axial skeleton contains and supports our organs and as such is less mobile; its task is protec-*

figure | 3-2 |

The appendicular skeleton.

figure | **3-3** |

Bones of the arm and hand, including a side view of the wrist joint.

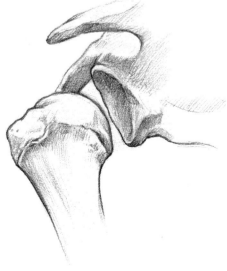

tion and support. *The appendicular skeleton provides leverage and motility to us; we can lift something overhead and run at the same time.* For the artist/animator, what are the basic shapes involved in drawing the forms and what is the range of motion available to them are the key questions. In looking at the human skeleton, we first need to determine what it can and cannot do. The first limiting factor for any part of the skeleton is what type of joint is connecting what types of bones together. Some joints, such as the sutures of the skull and cartilage adhesion of breastbone to rib are immobile, whereas the spine, with its cushiony discs between vertebrae, has some minor mobility. The wrists and ankle carpal and tarsal bones have plane joints with ligaments limiting the movement (*ligaments* are bone-to-bone attachments, versus *tendons*, which connect large muscle masses to bone).

Knees and the humerus/ulnar joints are hinge joints, limited to a simple swinging out or in motion.

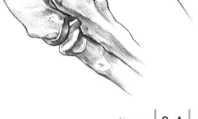

figure | **3-4** |

Knee joint and elbow joint.

The radius bone of the lower arm attaches by pivot to the humerus, somewhat like a miniature ball and socket, whereas the hip joint is a true ball and socket joint.

The radius to carpal joint is a type of ball and socket joint with limited range of motion (vertical), with the interlocking space ellipsoidal rather than circular.

Each of these shows a range of motion, with the ball and socket having the greatest range and the other joints somewhat less, depending upon the type. Fingers have saddle (thumb) and condyloid (first line of knuckles) joints, which have some circular motion available, in addition to a hinge-like action. Where the

figure | **3-5** |

Shoulder as example of a ball and socket joint.

figure | 3-6 |

The radius bone connection to the
carpal bones of the hand.

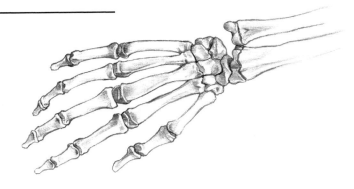

skull attaches to the uppermost cervical vertebrae
(the atlas, or cervical
one vertebra) allows a
forward/backward and
sideways tilting or rocking
motion. Underneath this is the second cervical vertebra (axis vertebra) that, in concert with
the atlas vertebra, gives us the ability to swivel our head.

Headbone

In a survey of the bones, it is customary to start with the skull, and we'll follow suit. There is
no doubt about the fascination the shape of the skull holds for humans. It is so
prominent in the shape and function of the face and head that one can
literally say these are just modified skulls, as far as artists are concerned. Because we so readily associate the skull with mortality, it
has become a metaphor for death and other similar themes, artis-
tically and socially. *As we mature from infant to adult, the lower
portions of the skull dramatically increase in size relative to the top
(cranial) portion of the skull.* As the skull houses the brain, it is
most important to our survival. A brief examination of the parts
of the skull is as follows. First the cranium, a composite of eight
bones sutured together, houses the brain, and is longer than it is
high and wide, rather like an egg flattened at both ends and
sides. It dominates the shape of the head.

At the front is a round part called the frontal bone, which rises
above the eyebrow ridges (superciliary crests) that protect the eyes
(see figure 3-7). At the outside, these descend to meet the zygomatic (cheek) bones (see figure 3-7). On the sides, the temporal
bones descend to the zygomatic arch, which moves forward to meet
the cheekbone (*zygomatic*). The lower jaw fits into a hollow at the
root of the zygomatic arch, allowing its hinge and sideways motion.
The ridges above the eye sockets end in a slight bowl called the glabel-
la, right above the root of the nose.

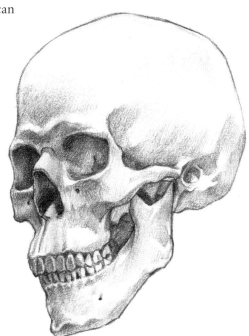

figure | 3-7 |

The human skull.

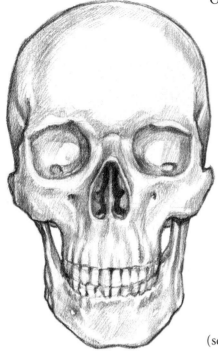

figure | **3-8** |

The human skull, front view.

Our nose starts with the nasal bone, a wedge perhaps an inch in length, and ends with cartilage. The zygomatic bones themselves form the shelf of the cheek, and part into three spurs that run along the outside of the brow, toward the temporal spur above the lower jaw, and to the nose, forming the lower orbital (eye socket) shape. *Of all the bones to which the artist must pay attention, this one ranks near the top.*

Our upper jaw, called the maxilla, is composed of two bones (the maxillae), which house the upper teeth, and lie beneath the zygomatic bones on the side. Where they join in front, underneath the nasal (nose) cavity, a sharp, upward-directed bit of bone (the nasal spine) intrudes into the nasal opening. Underneath, the lower jaw (mandible) juts to form a wide margin at the rear, narrowing to the front, descending angle wise from back to front downwards (see figure 3-7). It contains the lower teeth, and is the primary form in the lowest portion of the head. Proportionally, the three great zones of the face are cranial (perhaps two-fifths), orbital/nose (between one- and two-fifths), and the area from the nose to the bottom of the lower jaw, longer than the orbital/nose area by a bit.

The ear resides on two lines running roughly from the eyebrow ridge to just below the nose, and horizontally back along the head and just behind the jaw line. Many artists place the ear too far forward, not realizing the true position of the lower jaw in relation to the skull.

Spineless?

We normally only see the spine at its uppermost reaches, at the bottom of the neck (cervical vertebrae) and the beginning of the upper back (thoracic vertebrae), and also along the center of the back to the sacral (lowest back) region. Landmarks of the spine are the bump of the seventh cervical vertebra where the neck and upper back meet, and the bumps of the middle spinal spurs along the middle back, depending upon the fat and musculature of the subject.

figure | 3-9 |

figure | 3-9 |

Back view of the human figure showing
the spine and other features.

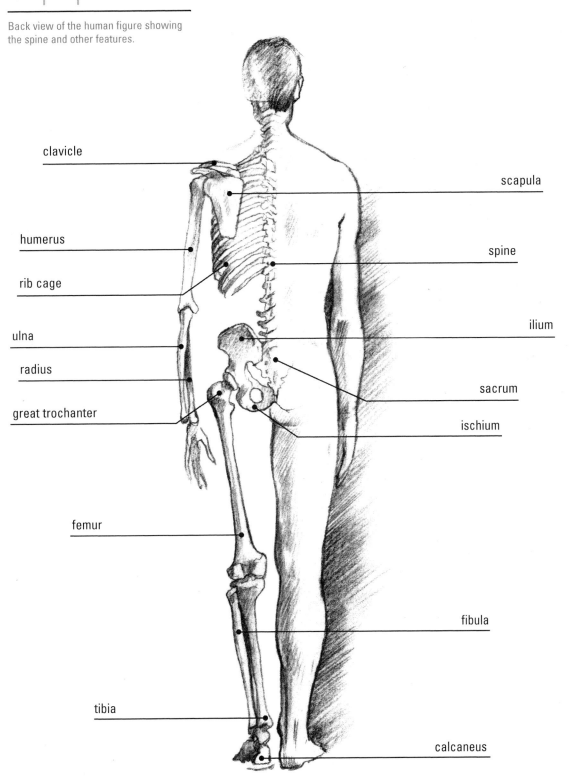

clavicle

scapula

humerus

spine

rib cage

ulna

ilium

radius

sacrum

great trochanter

ischium

femur

fibula

tibia

calcaneus

From the front, it is apparent that the vertebrae are larger the lower they are on the spinal column, which is logical, considering their increasing weight-bearing role. From the side, a significant set of curves appears which greatly influences how the figure is drawn. These form four curves starting at the top (cervical vertebrae), down the middle (thoracic vertebrae), and through the lower (lumbar) vertebrae.

In men, the lower curve outward is mild, but in most women, there is a pronounced outward curve of the lumbar vertebrae, contributing to the classic female form. The last curve is really the sacral bone, the base of the spine, which sits between the upper bones of the pelvis. Twenty-four vertebrae join in what is an amazing bit of engineering, a flexible multi-part tube, encasing the spinal column and simultaneously supporting and joining the head, shoulder/rib area, and pelvis. This total view of the vertebral system is incomplete without considering that the muscular attachments to upper, middle, and lower vertebrae vary in the amount of torque they will allow the body. In general, there is greater range of movement the higher you go on the spine.

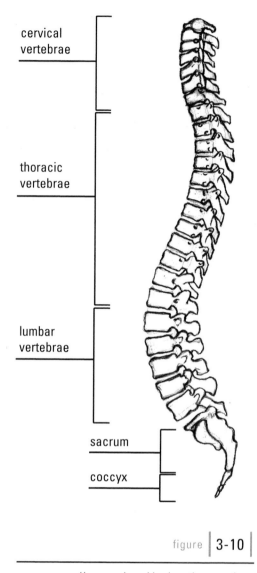

cervical vertebrae

thoracic vertebrae

lumbar vertebrae

sacrum

coccyx

figure | **3-10** |

Human spine, side view, three sections.

I'm Only Ribbing You

Attached to the spine is our rib cage. This egg-like form holds our upper internal organs and provides some of the support and connection to the musculature responsible for arm, back, and chest motion. It is tapered from bottom to top, and flattened front to back so that it is wider than deep (see figure 3-1). Twelve pairs of ribs form its shape, with the upper ten pairs connected by cartilage to the sternum, a flat bone in the front upper center of the rib cage. The top seven pairs are directly connected by individual cartilage pieces, and the eighth, ninth, and tenth pairs by straps of cartilage. The last two ribs are called floaters, precisely because they are not connected to the sternum. At the sternum, muscle tissue only thinly covers the bone, and its shape can often be seen in both men and women. Normal drawing errors for this part of the body are to make the top front portion of the rib cage too deep, producing an odd, box-like form that protrudes where the clavicles are (see figure 3-1). When drawing the human form, the artist should notice that the top of the sternum, called the manubrium, has two plates that meet the clavicle (collar) bones, and a central notch, the jugular notch, which is at the base of the neck. This forms another very noticeable landmark. Our necks (muscle/bone/surface) emerge from the top, kidney-shaped hole of the rib cage, between the clavicles in front and the trapezius muscles in back, a sort of diamond-shaped affair.

Male rib cages tend to be somewhat larger than female ones, and when comparing the rib cage to the pelvis, there is a marked reversal of size, with a broader pelvis in women and narrower in men, producing the classic straight male and figure eight female outlines. Ribs show on figures of men or women whose body fat is minimal and musculature not overly developed. Body-builders overlay enormous amounts of muscle tissue onto these bones, producing an odd, comic book appearance that has become widely overused as a template for character design. In truth, most body-builder rib cages are no bigger than an average person's. The ribs connect to the twelve thoracic vertebrae, and have a deep, vertical arch in front, up to the sternum. This space is filled with internal organs and covered with a strong wall of muscle tissue, but is still one of the vulnerable areas of the body. In size, the head is about two-thirds the height of the rib cage. In the frontal arch area, the descent of the ribs from the center is about sixty degrees for women and ninety degrees for men (see figure 3-1). The ribs themselves angle outwards from the center top to bottom and also down from the front top to bottom, producing a shallower, narrower top portion of the whole structure.

Living Girdle

Attached to the upper arm bone (humerus) and the clavicle (collarbone) is the scapula. Commonly called the wing bone, this is a triangularly shaped bone that is forward bending to accommodate the rib cage. It has a complex surface, and can articulate greatly outwards as the arms are raised (see figure 3-2). Numerous muscles attach to this important bone. Size-wise, it is about the length and width of a human hand, with the vertical face of the triangle nearest the spine. It nearly lines up with the sternum in front and has an overall appearance something like a pig's head, with snout (ball and socket joint for humerus) and ears (acromion and caracoid processes) (see figure 3-5). The former process can be seen at the top of the shoulder joint area, and is another surface landmark for artists. A scapula's spine is a bony process at the top, starting lower near the spine and rising to become the acromion process. Several major muscle groups make their way to this bony outcrop (see figure 3-5). In young children, this bone is often seen as a major back feature, whereas in adults it becomes more obscured by muscle and fat tissue. *The upper arm can only be raised to its full extent by the up and side sliding motion of the scapula. Below a horizontal position, the humerus chiefly does the arm-raising motion, but above the horizontal, the scapula performs the rest of the movement.*

Our collarbone, the clavicle, is one of the most vulnerable bones we have, and is the most frequently fractured bone of horse jockeys. Shaped like a very flattened horizontal letter "s," the clavicle connects the sternal region to the acromion process of the scapula. Neither connection is very strong. It is also about six inches long, similar to the sternum and scapula. The sternal connection is a quasi ball and socket joint, allowing the arm to move freely in a wide area. Near where the clavicle attaches to the acromion process is a roughened area for attachment of the deltoid (shoulder) muscle. *Women's collarbones tend to be less curved and shorter than men's.* Above and below the clavicle are landmark spaces or indentures (fossa). For artists, this is one of the most interesting and beautiful parts of the human body.

The Arms Race

Now we've reached the arms. By now you may be worried that you will never remember all of this information. All artists keep anatomy books and photo resource books available to reinforce and remind them of various parts of the anatomy story. By learning the major points given here, and *applying* them to the drawing exercises, remembering will be much easier.

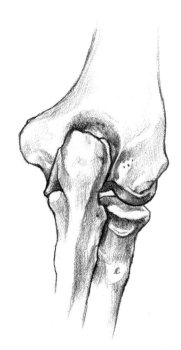

figure   **3-11**

Elbow joint, anterior view.

Arms are among the most familiar parts of the body for us, because they are usually visible, used frequently, and form a core part of social interaction. The upper bone of the arm is the humerus. It is the longest bone in the arm, and the heaviest. Its upper joint is a ball and socket joint with the scapula (see figure 3-5). The lower joint area of the humerus is another engineering marvel, with two types of joint attachments in one area. One, where the radius bone attaches to the humerus, is a sort of miniature ball and socket joint. The second, the attachment of the ulna and the humerus, is a modified sliding hinge-like joint.

When looking at the human figure, *the elbow appears to reach to about the bottom of the ribs.* This indicates the visual extent of the upper arm, and is a simple guideline to proportion when drawing people. *Because women generally have a shorter humerus than men, their elbow will strike slightly higher on the torso.* Our *elbow,* in actuality, comprises the lateral and medial epicondyles of the humerus and the hinge portion of the ulna, the olecranon (see figure 3-3). The medial (inner) epicondyle protrudes outward more than the lateral, and when combined with the olecranon, gives the characteristic squarish look to the elbow in the inside profile. From the outside profile the elbow appears more pointed (see figure 3-3). This represents a challenge to the artist to accurately portray this body area when in action, as the look changes from one aspect to another.

We have already mentioned the lower arm, which consists of two bones: the ulna and the radius. The lower arm represents a unique visual problem for artists, because these two bones change relative position to one another depending upon whether the radius rotates inward (pronation) or remains directed outward (supination). Because the radius is attached to the humerus by a small ball and socket arrangement, it is mobile in rotation mode, whereas the ulna, whose larger end is hinged to the humerus as well, moves in a limited up-down fashion. When combined, these two motions change the muscular shape of the lower arm considerably. We have seen frequent errors in drawing this body area in both student work and professional animation. In relaxed arm mode, with your arm hanging by your side, the radius will always be in front. If seen in a kind of x-ray fashion, the bones will appear to cross in a long "X" in pronation. This is one area that considerable life-drawing experience will help greatly.

Give Me a Hand!

It appears that many artists avoid drawing hands (and feet) because of their complexity and sheer difficulty in rendering. In fact, although complex in some ways, the extremities have certain patterns and overall shapes that make drawing them quite feasible. The hand forms a kind of wedge form that changes from being thick at the joint with the lower arm to thin at the ends of the phalanges (fingers).

At the arm joint, the small carpal bones cluster together to form a solid beginning to the hand and a place for a viable joining with the radius bone, which is much larger at this end than at its link to the humerus. The carpals together nest in such a way as to conjoin the ellipsoidal scoop at the end of the radius, while the small terminal bump of the ulna only helps support the joint indirectly (see figure 3-6). From the carpals, the metacarpals fan out in rather

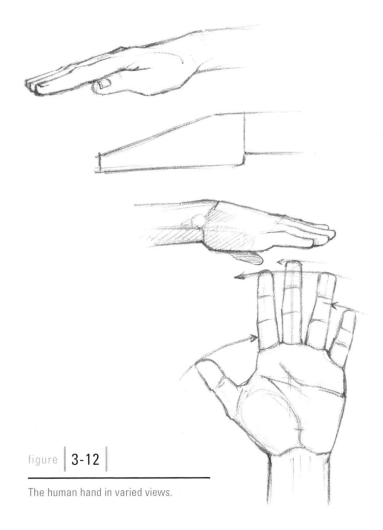

figure | **3-12** |

The human hand in varied views.

straight lines, with the fingers adding three more bones and the thumb two more. This shortening of the thumb, combined with the bend of the metacarpal bones and fingers, allows the thumb to be opposable. *It should be noted that the end of the thumb does not reach to the second knuckle of the index finger.* On the outside of the hand, the little finger starts lower than the other fingers and only extends to midway on the ring finger's second joint. In the center of the hand, the middle finger has somewhat longer segments, and is about a half-segment longer than the index and ring fingers. *The fingers form a curve ranging from the little finger, going up to the middle finger, and descending steeply to the thumb.* At each joint, the larger surfaces formed by the enlarged knuckle effect are sometimes overdone by eager character designers. Finger segments form a three to two ratio; that is, the second joint is 2/3 the length of the first joint, and the end or third joint is 2/3 the length of the second joint.

Feet

Feet are probably the most avoided area of the body for artists, and yet in many ways they are one of the easiest areas to draw. *As in the hands, the feet are wedge-like in appearance from a side view,* and start from a group of clustered bones called the tarsals. These bones are larger and obviously made for weight bearing, as opposed to the carpals of the hand, which are more generally functional. The tibia, the larger weight-bearing lower leg bone, lies directly above the talus and calcaneus (heel) bones. These provide a simple transfer of body mass to the foot, and including the cuboid, both support above and help transfer the stress forward.

The calcaneus lies along the outside of the foot (think *footprint*) and the cuboid is responsible for leading to the outside two metatarsal bones. The talus literally gives us the ability to move the ankle joint, with limited up and down motion (dorsa-flexion), pointing (plantarflexion, which flexes the main tendons in the sole of the foot), and inversion (in-pointing) and eversion (out-pointing). After the tarsals, which provide a curved archway toward the front, come the long metatarsals, with the big toe metatarsal shorter than the others. These culminate in the phalanges, with two visible for the big toe and three for the other four. Landmarks on the inside of the foot are the joint of the first metatarsal to the big toe, the head of the talus and tubercle of the navicular (on the inside of the foot), and the tuberosity of metatarsal five on the outside. Including the malleoli of each lower leg bone (ankle bones), these provide the main "bumps" for artists to look at when drawing a foot (see figure 3-13). *Sizes of feet are about a head's length from the heel to the start of the big toe, with the toes adding extra length past that.* Frankly, it is rare to have any other than the anklebones show up for any animation, but knowledge of these basic forms can give an edge to designing and planning character design quirks.

figure | 3-13 |

Bones of the foot, in two views.

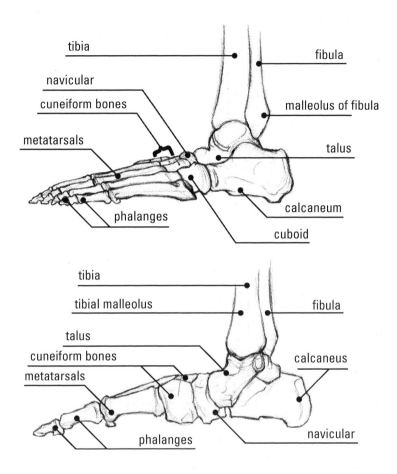

tibia

fibula

navicular

malleolus of fibula

cuneiform bones

metatarsals

talus

phalanges

calcaneum

cuboid

tibia

fibula

tibial malleolus

talus

cuneiform bones

calcaneus

metatarsals

phalanges

navicular

Pelvic Stories

Back up to the center is the fulcrum of the body, the *pelvis. In essence all action, balance, and large dependent motion derive from the pelvis.* The pelvis is actually constructed from several bones: the sacrum (at the base of the spine), the large iliac bones (top bones), and the ischial bones (at the bottom, with holes in them). Together they constitute the spinal and leg attachments for the skeleton.

Male and female pelvises differ, and this greatly contributes to the sexual dimorphism, or gender-influenced differences that we see in human bodies and their shapes. From the front, in a shape like a flared open bowl form, the upper hipbones clearly flare out beyond the smaller frontal ischia. In conjunction with the observation that in general the female trunk is longer than the male's, vis-à-vis the total body length, we find the pelvis in fact a bit shorter. However, *in women, the pelvis is wider and deeper, and more arched where the lumbar conjunction with the sacrum occurs, while in general leaning more forward.* We also observe the lumbar vertebrae thrusting outward in women, as has been mentioned before. *Most women have a wider sacrum, as well. The hips are further apart as a result of all this in women versus men, and interestingly, the widest point for women occurs below the hip, at the gluteal (buttock) fold. All this tends to give women greater curvature, lower body emphasis in size, and longer flanks.*

Pelvises are about the same length as the human head. They are the attachment locations for the upper leg bones (femurs) at a large, scooped out ball and socket joint, the acetabulum. This joint occurs more than halfway down and is well under the outer margin of the ilium. *When looking at a male pelvis, the front "bump" (anterior superior iliac spine) of the upper pelvic bone lies on the same plane as the pubis below. In the female, it is forward of the pubis.*

figure | **3-14** |

The human pelvis.

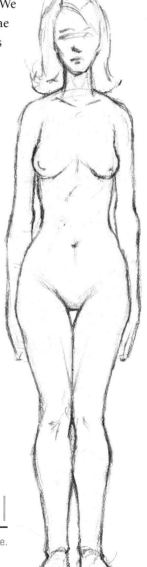

figure | **3-15** |

Generic female human figure.

A Leg Up

We finally arrive at the legs. Our upper leg bone is the longest and heaviest bone in the body. Anatomists can closely estimate the height of a person from this bone alone. It is usually about twice as long as a human head. Other than at the upper outside hip area and at the knees, the femur is completely buried by soft tissue. *You can see from figure 3-2, which shows the entire human skeleton, that the femur leans in from hip to knee. Even in the male figure this is true, and more so in the female, due to their wider pelvis. The gait of each is affected by this phenomenon; a kind of knock-kneed walk is more obvious is women, and the pelvis appears to rotate more obviously as women walk. The male leg bones are longer in relation to their trunk, in general, than in women.* At the top of the leg, where it joins the pelvis in our hip area, a projection of the femur, called the great trochanter, pushes out. This is the male's widest point. The femur attaches to the pelvis over halfway down, at the base of the ilium, in a ball and socket joint. At the base where the femur ends and joints the tibia and fibula in the knee joint, a great swelling in the condyles and epicondyles occurs. These swellings of the bone laterally give a large surface for the joint, which is a hinge joint, to support the body weight (see figure 3-2). In front of this joint floats the patella, the knee bone, which glides over the notch in front of the femur base called the patellar surface. The patella is locked to the tibia by the patellar ligament, which is an extension of the top middle quadriceps muscle. Behind the knee bone is a pad of fat, and this gives us less detail of the bones of the joint area by partly covering them.

Now that we've covered the top of the leg, let's complete our tour of the skeleton by examining the lower leg. The larger of the two bones (and slightly longer in length) is the tibia, which is the inner (medial) bone of the lower leg. It generally is about fifteen inches long. At the knee joint, its massive head forms the base for the hinge joint of femur and tibia. When looking straight on at the skeleton, we can see that, whereas the femur angles in toward the center, the lower leg bones are much more straight up and down. The front (anterior) edge or crest of the tibia is a landmark for the artist, and curves slightly (see figure 3-2). At the outer side of the lower leg, the fibula starts a little lower on the outer knee area, not actually touching the femur. It acts as an outer support mechanism, and ends at the ankle in the lower anklebone (malleolus) that is the outer (lateral) part of the ankle hinge motion. The malleolus of the tibia, which ends somewhat higher than that of the fibula, is the inner "container" of the ankle joint. *A good tip for artists is that the outer curve of the upper part of the lower leg is higher than the inner curve, and the outer ankle is lower than the inner ankle.*

figure | 3-16 |

Human lower leg curve locations.

Part two of this fairly long chapter is devoted to the human musculature, and in concert with our examination of the skeleton, will give a good, broad overview of anatomy for the beginning artist and animator.

Muscle Beach

Now that we have established the framework on which the muscles hang, we can look at each area of the body and see what major muscles are involved and how they might affect both mechanics and shape for the artist.

It should be noted that muscles tend to arrange themselves in opposite functional pairings; what we mean by this is that in moving a body part one way with one set of muscles, there must be the necessary means to return that body part to its original position. This gives us *antagonist* muscle groups, such as the quadriceps on the front of the upper leg and the hamstrings on the back (the first are extensors, the second flexors). Each pulls the leg in an opposite direction. Often muscles will move more than one item of the body; the biceps can flex the arm and also participate in rotating the forearm. Muscles end in tough, fibrous tissue called tendons, and it is that tissue that connects the muscle to bone. *When in operation, muscles flex and thus change shape. So we cannot speak of just a single shape of a muscle; the shape of the muscle depends upon what it is doing.*

When we explored the skeletal system, it probably became apparent that how the human body moves is directly linked to the rigid skeleton and how it is put together. A human body is restricted by this bioengineering, as are all other animals with endoskeletons. The musculature, although important in motion (paramount for animators), has perhaps more to do with shape for the artist. Because the extreme shapes of superheroes and body-builders are often seen as examples of the human body, the idea of what is normal can sometimes be distorted. We recommend that you learn anatomy as it is for the general population, thereby ensuring that your drawings will contain character development other than muscle-bound types.

Muscles of the Head

Attaching the head to the body at the front sides are the sternomastoids. They form the familiar cording on either side of the throat area, and attach to the top of the sternum with one head and on the clavicle with the second at their base, and on the temporal bone of the skull. It should be noted here that *the throat is marked by the thyroid cartilage, the familiar Adam's apple, which is more prominent in males than in females.*

Just above this is the virtually unseen hyoid bone, a floating semi-oval that is involved in speech. Several small muscles lie underneath the jaw, and form a gentle curve from chin to neck (see figure 3-18). Above, from cheekbone to jaw, sits the masseter muscle, which, along with cheek fat, fills the space. It is used in chewing and opening and closing the lower jaw.

figure | 3-17 |

Human musculature, front view.

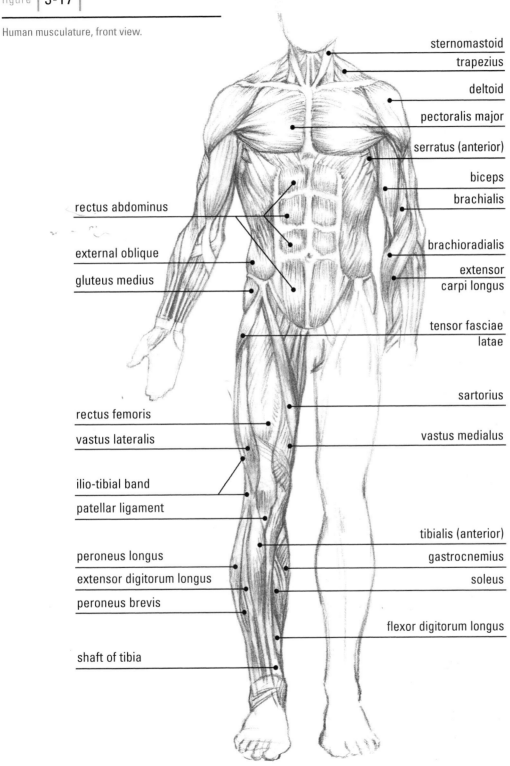

- sternomastoid
- trapezius
- deltoid
- pectoralis major
- serratus (anterior)
- biceps
- brachialis
- brachioradialis
- extensor carpi longus
- tensor fasciae latae
- sartorius
- vastus medialus
- tibialis (anterior)
- gastrocnemius
- soleus
- flexor digitorum longus

- rectus abdominus
- external oblique
- gluteus medius
- rectus femoris
- vastus lateralis
- ilio-tibial band
- patellar ligament
- peroneus longus
- extensor digitorum longus
- peroneus brevis
- shaft of tibia

figure | 3-18 |

Shape of the human throat
and facial musculature.

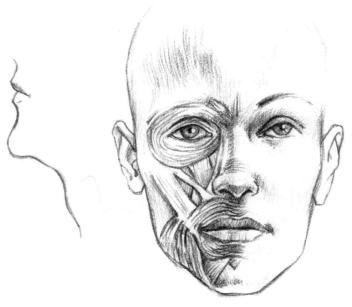

Circling the mouth and both eyes are the orbicularus muscles (one for each area). Other than the mentalis of the front chin prominence and the triangularis on either side (see figure 3-18), most facial muscles are too thin to dominate the bone or cartilage structures of the head. The nose and ears are primarily cartilage, and are shown in figure 3-19.

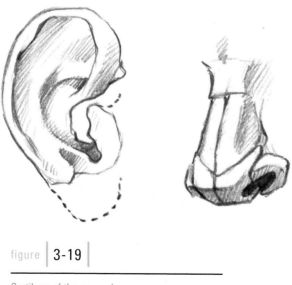

figure | 3-19 |

Cartilage of the ear and nose.

The head is supported in back to a great extent by the top of the trapezius muscle, which, when viewed from the front, the visual appearance of the incline of the muscle from neck to shoulder fills the gap with its gentle slope upward.

Joining it are several more internalized muscles that need not concern the artist except to be aware that they also fill the gap between the trapezius and sternomastoids and help support the head.

figure | 3-20 |

Musculature of the human, back view.

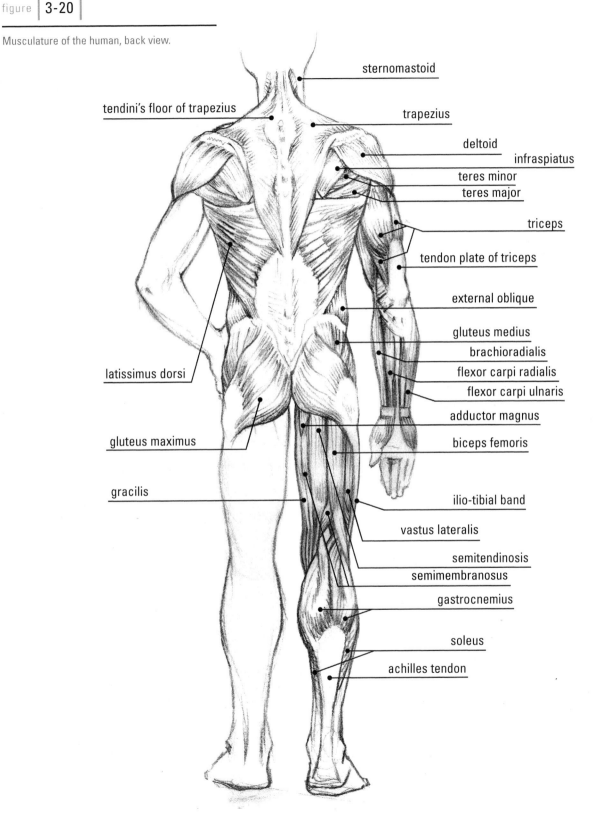

sternomastoid

tendini's floor of trapezius

trapezius

deltoid

infraspiatus

teres minor

teres major

triceps

tendon plate of triceps

external oblique

gluteus medius

brachioradialis

flexor carpi radialis

flexor carpi ulnaris

adductor magnus

biceps femoris

latissimus dorsi

gluteus maximus

gracilis

ilio-tibial band

vastus lateralis

semitendinosis

semimembranosus

gastrocnemius

soleus

achilles tendon

Meanwhile, Back at the Ranch…

Moving back to the trapezius, we realize that it is essentially a back muscle, with two wing-like heads (see figure 3-20). It overtly attaches to the spine of the scapula, and progresses downwards to the center of the back on either side of the spine. It forms one of the major landmarks of the back. In the tendon separating the two halves of the trapezius, one can see the bump of the seventh and last cervical (neck) vertebra, which is another back landmark. Beside the top portion of the trapezius, and attaching to the other side of the scapular spine, is the cap of the shoulder, the deltoid. Each *deltoid* covers from front to back over the shoulder top, and so is marked both in front and in back on the figure (see figures 3-17 and 3-20). *It is usually, but not always, more pronounced in the male figure.* Along its outer edge is a subtle double curve, often overlooked even by good artists. Filling the space between the deltoid and trapezius are several smaller muscles that inhabit the hollowed out area of the scapula. The infraspinatus dominates the inner area and the teres major shows up as the top of the curve we normally associate with the lats, the latissimus dorsi, which is largely apparent in bodybuilders. This muscle overlays and completely covers the bottom half of the back, moving sideways and upward to the humerus and downward to several rib and spinal attachments. Next to the spine it becomes a flat tendon sheath, descending to a point at the base of the sacrum. Along the spine are the sacrospinalus muscles, lying alongside and forming a parallel ridge on either side. *Finally at the base outside, just over the pelvic crest, we see the flank pad of the external obliques just peeking out. These are far more pronounced in the male figure, practically unseen in females other than athletes or body-builders.* We will talk more about the external obliques when we get to the front of the torso.

Up and Front

Now that we've reviewed the back of the figure, we come to the more familiar front torso area. As we said before, the trapezius muscles reach over the shoulder tops to visually connect the outer shoulder to the neck. Immediately in front at the top are the clavicle bones, and attaching to each are the front portions of the deltoids (see figure 3-17). Connecting from below and covering the upper portion of the torso in "squarish" fashion are the pectorals. These are the surface pectorals, and they also attach to the humerus and centrally to the sternum. They define this portion of the male anatomy, and along with the breast tissue, the female upper torso as well. In the female the breasts lay on top of the chest muscles, usually found between the third and sixth ribs, and point somewhat outwards. The nipple, also aligning outwards, can be found at about the fifth rib height. The upper portion of the breast is flattish, segueing into the pectoral muscle in a smooth transition, whereas the lower breast area folds over the muscles, attaching by fascia to them. Protruding from the lower side and backwards is a bulge of fatty tissue, the auxiliary tail, making the breast look something like a large comma in shape. Depending upon the person, the female breast may be more conical or more rounded. Because it is soft tissue, fat and glandular in nature, it is affected by gravity. As such, it will flatten when a female is reclining on her back, be ellipsoidal when upright, or pendulous when hanging down. The male nipple is found just below the fourth rib. In the male, there is only a small, thin disc of fat below the nipple.

From the outside rib area, downward to the flanks adjoining the pelvic girdle, are the external obliques (see figure 3-17). These are flatter at the top and interweave with underlying muscles with the ribs, finally ending up at the bulge of the flank pads just above the pelvic iliac spine. Covering the central area from the sternal notch down to the groin is the rectus abdominis, a four-part muscle with a central tendinous separation (see figure 3-17). This covers and retains the vital organ area of the body, and can become lax and pendulous with extra weight and age, giving us the "potbelly" look.

Taking Up Arms

Now looking at the arms fleshed out, we see familiar forms such as the biceps (see figure 3-17). This is the front flexor of the upper arm, and it is flatter and longer when relaxed, and bunched with an obvious tendon root when flexed. Between the biceps and the back of the arm is the not-often-seen brachialis (obvious only in athletes and body-builders), echoing the biceps in general direction. Behind and powering the extensor half of the upper arm muscles are the triceps. Higher than the biceps in front, these cover the back of the upper arm and form three heads; a long head on the upper inside, a medial head on the joint end inside, and a lateral head on the outside. The lower portion ends in a flat tendon sheath that wraps around the elbow.

On the lower arm, descending from the humerus between the triceps and brachialis, are the brachioradialis (linked to the radius bone, hence the name) and extensor carpi radialis longus, a long name for a muscle that helps move the fingers and runs parallel to the brachioradialis. These form the familiar dip at the elbow/forearm where the separation between them and the outside muscles of the forearm occurs. Outside, we find several muscles dropping from top to bottom and linking with the hand. These include the extensor carpi ulnaris, which glides along the ulna and helps form the top of the groove on that side of the lower arm. The large thenar muscles of the thumb and the hypothenar muscles of the outer hand give the largest bulk tissue to this extremity (see figure 3-17).

Leggo!

At last, we reach the leg. After examining this area, we'll take a brief look at some animals and make educated guesses about aliens. As can be expected, the leg muscles are more massive than the arm's, due to the weight-bearing role they play. Starting at the hip, and lying diagonally from outside to inside downwards, is the longest muscle of the body, the sartorius (see figures 3-17 and 3-20). It provides the border between the large quadriceps of the upper front thigh and the smaller adductors reaching into the pubic tubercle. The quadriceps themselves reveal one buried and three visible muscles, with the central rectus femoris taking the visual emphasis. It tapers to a large tendon that overlaps the patella and connects to the bump on the top front of the tibia. On the outside, the vastus lateralis (outer quad) defines the perimeter shape of the upper leg, and the vastus medialis (inner quad) slips past the sartorius strap and gives us a pronounced curve at the inner knee area. Above the hip socket, the gluteus medius bulges, and at the socket the smaller tensor fasciae latae is visible, especially in dancers. Behind the pelvis, the gluteus maximus completely dominates the hindquarters, bounded on the bottom edge by fat and a band of fibrous tissue, giving us the gluteal furrow between it and the upper leg (all shown in figures 3-17 and 3-20). The long gracilis muscle defines the final inner border of the thigh. At the back of the upper leg, the hamstrings (semitendinosus and semimembranosus) dive down from the buttock, slender compared to the quads, and connecting past the outer knee to the lower leg. At the border between the quads and hamstrings on the outside leg is a long cleft occupied by the ilio-tibial band, a tough tendinous tissue.

The lower leg anterior (back) is overwhelmingly occupied by the flexor gastrocnemius, whose two heads end in the large tendon that becomes the Achilles tendon above and behind the heel of the foot. This slender extension of the tendon provides the total shape of that part of the back leg. The inner (medial) head of the gastrocnemius is slightly lower than the outer (lateral) head. Combined with the opposite higher/lower levels of the malleoli of the fibula and tibia, we get a valuable diagram for drawing legs, as seen in figure 3-17. Below the gastrocnemius, sandwiched between the tibia and the Achilles tendon, is the pillow of the soleus muscle. On the inside of the lower leg this provides a second slight convex curve, and helps push the lower outside out as well. Along the tibia lies the large tibialis muscle, diving to the base of metatarsal one. At the outer border, the peroneus longus gives us the last outer curve of the lower leg, and two other extensors fill the remaining space and connect finally to the metatarsals and phalanges. The total effect is of a jaunty curve from outer knee to inner ankle (all shown in figures 3-17 and 3-20). The foot has a fat pad underneath for cushioning our weight, and this spills out laterally as we press our feet down.

This concludes a somewhat tedious but very useful trip through a basic artist's examination of the human anatomy. Proportionally, trying to memorize head lengths for various body parts is usually not a good idea, since there is a great deal of variety among human beings, but some general rules of thumb are as follows. An average female stands seven to seven and a half heads tall, with a midpoint at nearly the top of the groin area. Males are similarly seven and a half heads, with a midpoint slightly lower in the groin. Elbows touch the base of the ribs (which are one and a half heads tall), and hands brush about midthigh. On the male, from head to chin and chin to nipple is about equal, nipple to navel one head also, and navel to base of groin one head. In the female, the long flank gives us a measurement from base of buttock to rib equal to base of rib to base of chin.

On the head, there is about one eye's width between the eyes, with the total head width about five eyes. From pupil to pupil to base of nose is a very rough equilateral triangle. The upper lip is usually shorter than the space from lower lip to chin; from eyebrow to base of nose is about equal to base of nose to base of chin. This last measurement is sometimes not quite true in petite female faces.

The head is about three units high to four units long, i.e., a three to four ratio, and five units long to six units tall, a five to six ratio.

The distance from top of head to base of buttocks is about four head units; the upper leg runs about two heads long; and the lower leg is about a half-head less.

A reminder: these are very general measurements. Observation is key in producing valid and believable figures.

CRITTERS

At this point, we want to simply point out some basic similarities (and a few differences) between human and similar animal anatomies. The most obvious overlap is the skeleton. Looking at various simplified animal skeletons in relation to a human skeleton, we can see that the rib cage, spine, and often the pelvis provide commonalities that, when drawing, are produced in almost the same way.

Despite such additions as trunks, ears, throat wattles, and crests, etc., there is an overt *sameness* to these creatures. The vast majority of ground dwellers walk on all fours (*quadrupeds*), and most of these walk literally on their toes (*digitigrades*). Two exceptions are bears and people (*plantigrades*); they walk flat-footed. Bats use modified finger bones to produce wings; birds use the whole arm bone assembly for wings, sacrificing four-legged locomotion for the glories of flight. The gaits of animals can, however, differ due to subtle changes in parts of the bone structure. A prehistoric bison's run is constrained by where the tall vertebral spines are located. Attachments of various muscles, combined with leg length, will give different freedoms in the gait. Differing species have variations in anatomical proportions; this can also be seen, for example, in large predatory dinosaurs. A Giganotosaurus, the extinct South American rival in size to T-Rex, will clearly have, with its massive leg bones and multi-ton body weight, a less svelte run than the gracile, newly discovered Allosaurus-like theropods of west Africa. Smaller predators similarly begin to look pretty speedy, more like ostriches and roadrunners. In general, you will note that the pelvis in animals that walk on all fours is level and rather different from our own bowl-shaped affair. This allows the spine to align along the direction of motion and for the hind legs and forelegs to efficiently move in concert, as well. Sea dwellers move sometimes in dissimilar ways, yet look much alike. A shark moves by sideways undulations of the body while a dolphin moves forward by up-and-down motions. In these sea creatures, legs are now flippers, useful for navigation and some propelling at slower

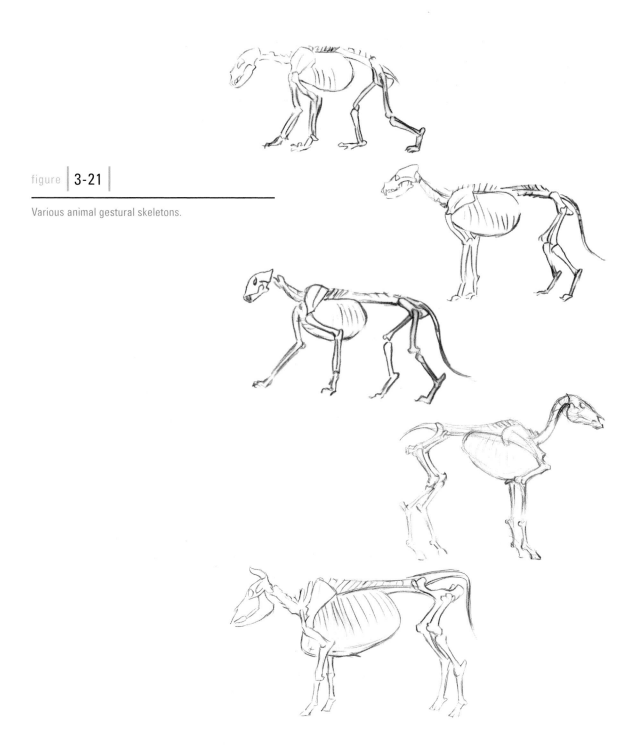

figure | 3-21 |

Various animal gestural skeletons.

speeds. It appears that the prehistoric plesiosaurs may have used a four-flippered variety of propulsion now unknown among animals, an alternating back and front scoop and push. Yet all these have, still, a backbone, skull, rib cage, and pelvic area, although the pelvis can become much diminished in many sea creatures. On land, stride length, weight, center of gravity, and balance give the elephant a ponderous, lock-kneed walk/run and the cheetah a fabulous, lithe and outstretched run. The massive guts of many herbivores are due to the need for lengthy entrails to digest difficult vegetation, hence their potbellied look. Flyers can be fast and furious, like the hummingbird, or slow and graceful, as in a vulture. A couple of examples of locomotion are shown in figure 3-22.

figure | 3-22 |

Two types of animal locomotion.

For animals like insects, the skeleton is on the outside, an exoskeleton. Because of this, their size is greatly constrained; there is a limit to how much mass the small muscle attachments and hardened shells can contain and move. Insects the size of a fist are rare and don't move very rapidly. In prehistoric times, there were huge millipedes that were a few feet long, by virtue of segmentation. The locomotion of such animals is stiffer and, in the case of spiders, rather random compared to skeletal animals. In the sea, lighter gravitational loads allowed some greater leeway in size, with trilobites and their ilk becoming upwards of a yard in length. Cephalopods, such as squid, having no skeletal restrictions and buoyed by the water, can reach fifty feet in length. Some giant octopi off the coast of Alaska dwarf a human being. Their grace and strength are useless out of the water, though, just as a bird's advantage in the air ceases when it has a broken wing. Life forms that dwell on the sea floor, such as anemones, seem quite remote from us, despite having some structures in common.

Using these sources for the invention of alien life forms can be exciting and also confusing. In another venue, we will talk at greater length about this challenge. However, we would like to emphasize that using derived, real structures that we are familiar with in constructing a lifeform that we have never seen can give the latter a realness and functional validity that sometimes is lacking in some game and film design. The reference to flying dragons being a case in point, drawing animals should follow a few simple rules to start. If they have a like number of limbs as us, then it follows that they can use a similar skeletal system as well. If sea dwelling or air dwelling, then forms from those realms can give clues as to possible construction. Avoid constructions that clearly are nonfunctional hybrids if you can, such as extra limbs on an ordinary human torso. Wings and flippers developed in response to need; tacking them on without giving a good reason why (or a clear idea *how* it works) is cheap design. *Remember this: whatever you have designed and drawn, as a static character model, must now be able to move, and move authentically. Animation is about movement.* Just mastering the minimal anatomic information in this chapter takes a good deal of time, but the rewards are greater freedom and authenticity in your animation.

CHAPTER SUMMARY

Knowledge of the basics of human and animal anatomy and biological structure are important for developing key design elements for the animator and character designer. The structure of the skeleton and the engineering of the musculature form the foundation for human/creature locomotion and physical abilities. Understanding the relationship of anatomy to observational drawing is an important factor in creating plausible, dynamic character movement.

exercises

1. Review bone and muscle charts for humans and various animals, and practice learning the names of bones and muscle groups.

2. Review bone and muscle charts for humans and various animals, and practice locating identical bones and muscle groups.

3. Utilizing photographs of hands and feet in various poses, create an overlay drawing of the bone structure of each appendage on tracing paper, as if creating an x-ray view of these body parts.

4. Utilizing photographs or your own drawings of the human figure in various poses, create an overlay drawing of the skeletal structure of each figure on tracing paper, as if creating an x-ray view of the body.

5. Draw the human figure in different poses as skeletal gestures. Simplify the rib cage and pelvis into basic geometric structures.

6. Dimensional visualization is a useful tool for building your comprehension level of anatomy. Using oil or polymer clay (such as Super Sculpey®), sculpt an arm, leg, or torso, lying in the muscles independently before overlaying with skin. Try using these sculptures as drawing references.

in review

1. What are the axial and appendicular skeletons, and what is the difference between the two?

2. Name two hinge joints and two ball and socket joints of the human skeleton.

3. Digitigrade refers to what form of locomotion? Plantigrade refers to what other mode of locomotion?

4. The height of a human head is in what approximate relationship to the total height of the male body? To the female body?

5. What are the three divisions in the human spine?

6. What is a biped? What is a quadruped?

sequences visited and revisited

objectives

Learn the concept of sequence drawing and how to refine these drawings

Acquire an understanding of the relationship of perspective to sequence drawing

Comprehend the relationship of 2D animation to sequence drawing

Develop an understanding of key-framing and sequence drawing and how they are interdependent

Gain an understanding of the use of live models for sequence studies for animators

introduction

Once you have begun to have a comfort level in drawing the figure, a new use for short sketches emerges. This exercise is directly linked to using gestures and moderately developed contour drawings to describe a figure in action. We call this a *sequence drawing,* very similar to stop-action photography, where each significant step in the action is described by a photo or frame of film. Eadweard Muybridge's sequential photographic studies revolutionized our ideas about the movement of animals.

> ## ▶ Who the Heck Is This Muybridge Guy, Anyway?
>
> Eadweard Muybridge was an Englishman, born in Kingston, England in 1830. After a brief stint as a prospector in America, during which time he was severely injured, he went home to England, only to return to become a professional photographer. After establishing himself in this country, he was approached by Leland Stanford, former governor of California and a horse breeder. Stanford wanted to document whether a horse had all four feet off the ground at the same time while trotting (and also to increase the efficiency of his race horses, in general). Muybridge was able to prove, through a series of sequential photographs, that a horse's hooves are all four completely off the ground at certain stages of movement within the trot. Muybridge went on to do many sequential photographic series of animals and people in motion. To this day, artists and scientists use these photographic series as a resource.

Previous to the Muybridge studies, people had debated whether or not a horse had all four of its hooves off the ground at any point during a trot. It does; and this fact was verified with photographic evidence. For the first time, scientists and artists were able to view elements of human and animal action frozen in time. In sequence drawing, the principal parts of the action are drawn quickly as the model holds each part of the action for perhaps two minutes.

figure | 4-1 |

Gestural sequence drawings.

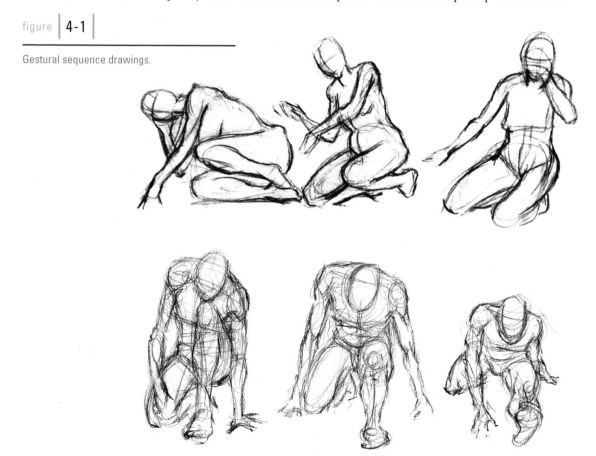

Sometimes the sequence is only three or four drawings, and sometimes it's longer. With some of the poses, it is a good exercise to see only the first and last (of a three-step sequence) and then try to draw the middle step by examining the other two drawings. This extrapolated drawing forces you to understand both the action dynamic and anatomical necessities for this action. Sequence drawings are similar to key-framing and breakdown drawings in animation, and their study is invaluable to being fluent at the former. *Sequence drawing, as a reference for animators, allows the movement of body parts to be plotted by position over time.* Working from the live model or a series of photographs, we can directly visualize how far a person's torso twists when throwing a left hook or track the position of a character's nose during a wild take. *You should try to retain the general size and proportion of the figure in each drawing, and should draw the line of action and continuous action lines connecting critical parts of the figure from one pose to the next.* This allows the artist see where the dynamic of the action is and to be able to follow the flow of the action.

figure | 4-2 |

Following the flow of action.

NOTE

Start from the Center

Pay particular attention to the axial skeleton/torso area, as this is where all other parts of the body radiate from and are dependent upon in any pose. If this central region twists, it is a certainty that the legs and arms are going to move in new and diverse directions from each other. The head, as well, will move in concordance with the torso, with the added possibility of extra twist because of the mobile atlas cervical vertebra. Position your drawings on your paper with the full set of poses spread horizontally so that they may be analyzed and scaled.

Analyzing human movement in sequence provides visual information on how to create accurate and believable motion in animated movement. To reiterate, a sequence drawing is like a "freeze-frame" snapshot of a particular activity or action. We have already talked about how using gesture drawings spaced apart in time can describe what something or someone is doing. What we are doing in sequence drawing exercises is rehearsing the frame-by-frame analysis that artists do when animating. The difference here is that this exercise is normally an output from life-drawing classes, rather than from a hired model or filmed activities. Even so, you can gain a great deal of knowledge and confidence by doing numerous sequences along with your other life-drawing studies.

Some useful exercises emphasize anatomical issues, like anatomical constraints on the motion of humans and other living things. One of the related comical errors that crops up in inexperienced animation is an action that is physically impossible, without the redeeming feature of exaggeration. This is also true in still images. Although there can be aesthetic considerations that can change proportion and articulation (see artists El Greco, Jean-Auguste-Dominique Ingres, and Michelangelo in old master compilations), this type of judgment should be left to art directors and concept artists when a project is being studied. Sound foundational use of anatomy and physics is the first step. These parameters can be stretched when there is a good reason to do so. What you should do is find out what the human body is actually capable of doing. To this end, some sequence exercises can be very helpful, because the actual physical limitations are expressed right in front of your eyes. Some sequence studies require a fairly athletic model that can hold difficult poses. These sequences are mostly designed to demonstrate some physical principal, such as torque or torsion in the torso, spine flexibility forward and backwards, leg extension, arm rotation, and so on.

figure | 4-3 |

Sequence drawing.

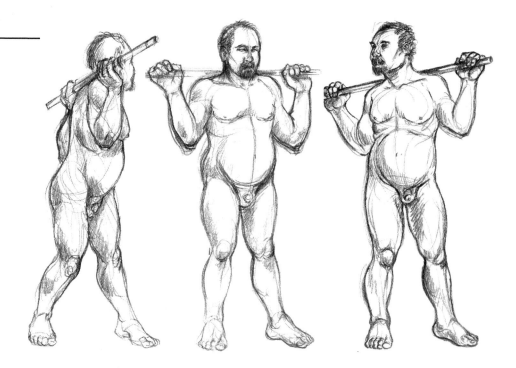

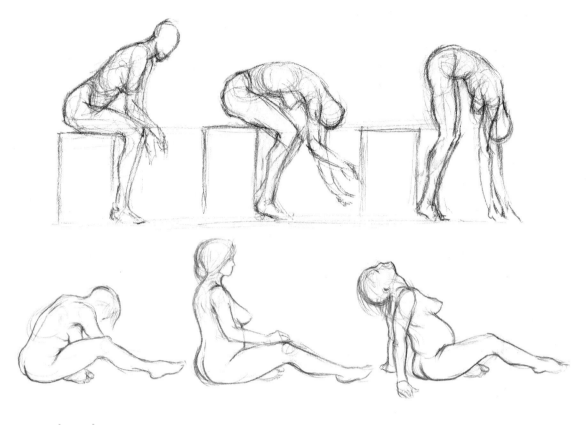

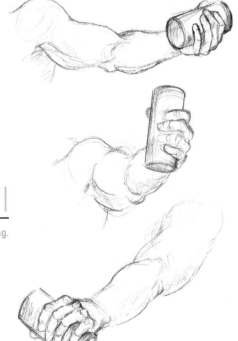

figure | 4-4 |

Sequence drawing.

figure | 4-5 |

Sequence drawing.

| NOTE |

Center of Gravity?

The center of gravity is the single point in a body (an object that has mass) upon which all gravitation forces are exerted and/or to which all matter is attracted. If the mean center of the weight and the center of gravity in a body are aligned, the body is balanced.

Let's put it this way: if the center of the weight in a person's body shifts away from its alignment with the central point at which the earth's gravity is pulling on their body, they tend to fall over.

WEIGHTY ISSUES

Center of gravity is also clearly shown in these poses, and it is sometimes very difficult for the live model to maintain balance without supports. The importance of the center of gravity becomes apparent when doing these sequence drawings or in sculpting maquettes (small sculptures that are preliminary versions of bigger ones). This concept involves how an animate or inanimate object remains stable.

figure | **4-6**

Sequence drawing.

Change in the center of gravity during motion can sometimes end with drastic results (such as the baby learning to walk and plopping backwards). If this is not taken into account, the "realness" of the activity can become questionable to the viewer. Characters that are top or bottom heavy, or machines that have multiple parts with weight and mobility can complicate what a student might consider "common sense" animation.

figure | 4-7 |

Top heavy and bottom heavy characters.

In these sequence exercises, it would be valuable to note where the center of gravity is and how it affects the motion or pose.

figure | 4-8 |

Problematic center of gravity.

WHOOPS!

TORSION, PHYSIOGNOMY, AND OTHER BIG WORDS

Again, sequence drawing exercises are useful in visually following where crucial anatomical parts are in each pose throughout an action. *For example, the hip joints and shoulder joints are key markers (we're talking "landmarks" again) for the human figure, and in actually marking them and following these marks with a line, you can see where the flow of the action is and how the figure conforms to this.*

figure | 4-9 |

Flow of action in a sequence drawing.

The action itself has a total directional flow, with the major body masses (or major components, if inanimate) indicating where the animator can draw a preparatory line to indicate the area to be filled later with sequential images. So the entire figure or object "directs" the animation by giving key points that, after being lined up, constitute a direction or action line.

Tracking and gauging anatomical elements is a crucial factor in animation for keeping motion and orientation constant over time. We are also concerned with believability and scale continuity, as well, and having a means of locating vital features is important.

Sequence drawings are also practical tools, which force you to analyze what elements are present in a sequence and project missing steps in that sequence. To this end, "fill in the blank" exercises can be done in several different ways. One exercise would be to have the model perform an action, and then hold only the beginning and end poses, forcing you to figure out what the missing middle step would look like. This exercise can be varied by having alternating poses missing, or by having two or more steps in between the first and last poses imagined and then drawn. To solve these exercises, the use of markers (head, shoulders, hips, knees, etc.) is of great value, as well as laying in a line of movement and some broad indications of rotation of the figure.

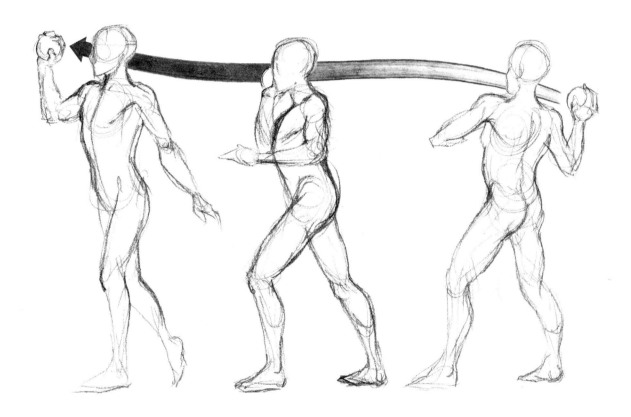

The obvious application to key-framing in animation cannot be over emphasized. Each drawing resembles a key frame, that is, drawings used by animators at "key" parts of a motion or activity, which limit and guide the action for the animator.

Rotation in space is also important to the animator. Rotational sequences from live figure reference allow practice in keeping physical proportions accurate over a drawing series. This is paramount in

| **NOTE** |

All animators know that they are their own best models. Don't hesitate to stand in front of a mirror to verify poses, walks, and facial expressions. Students in a class setting might tend to be shy about cavorting down a hallway to figure out a walk cycle, but frankly, it's one of the best ways to actually see how it works. Try it yourself!

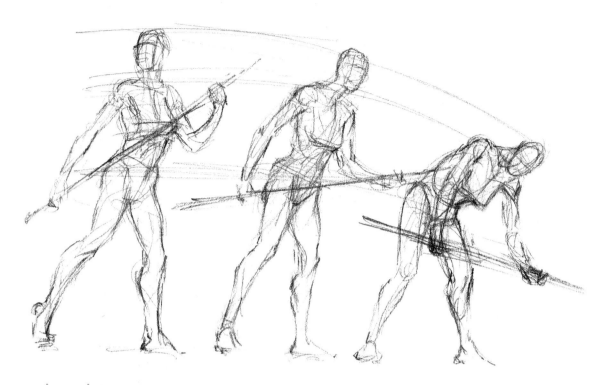

figure | 4-11 |

Markers for flow of action.

figure | 4-12 |

Sequence frames similar to key frames.

creating good animation skills. With the advent of computers, a wire-frame model of the figure or object can be constructed and then rotated to give any view wished by the animator. In traditional 2D animation, the animator must construct these views, which can require hours in the life-drawing studio. Even with computer-driven imagery, the ability to sketch a view of something in the concept stage greatly reduces the total development time of characters, objects, and scenes. These drawings can be used as a basis for further development. Sequence sketching often means having to extrapolate what something looks like in a different or foreshortened view. Having to draw a model in a straightaway pose, and then drawing the pose as though viewing it from different angles (and then verifying these drawings by moving to those points in the room) is a good way to see in the mind's eye. *Doing this shows that recording and understanding the torso, or core of the figure, is crucial to rotating the entire figure. The reason for this is readily apparent; the head, arms, and legs are dependent upon the torso for placement, and so if the torso is correctly drawn, then the rest of the figure is easier to understand. That is why starting with the head in drawing is not necessarily a good idea, since its value as a marker is much less complex and vital than the core of the figure.* This was made clear in the chapter on anatomy, where the technical attachments and actual placement and proportion of each of these elements were delineated.

As the torso itself is flexible due to the spine and attendant musculature, care must be taken to not render the torso as a stiff, wooden replica of the real thing. The flexibility of the spine introduces several possible modes of dependent and independent torsion for elements of the figure.

figure | **4-13**

Independent and dependent torsion (twist) in the figure.

A final complicating aspect is the fact that the shoulders are independently mobile (with scapula, clavicle, and shoulder joint), giving the figure another possible related set of poses and motions.

figure | 4-14 |

Independent movement of collarbones; working from a live model for key frames and sequence sketches.

Sequential rotation of the figure or an anatomical element (arm, leg, head, etc.) allows us to see a change in physiognomy over time: muscles shorten or elongate, mass and volume change or appear to change with the stretching and compression of tissue. Being aware of these things will give the artist an advantage when working in computer animation, because all of the changes in volume and shape must be carefully worked out mechanically rather than by fluid hand skills. If the artist keeps the character stiff, the whole naturalistic feel of the animation and its dynamism will be missing.

Sequence sketches give the artist a chance for another skill practice. This is scale, or being able to draw at the same scale repeatedly. Part of the goal is hand/eye coordination. Another goal is to be able to visually discern scale, so as to not introduce strange size aberrations in a scene. Animators are required to keep scale constant (when distance remains constant), that is, if character "A" is not moving toward or away from the viewer, then its scale shouldn't change arbitrarily. In cartoons involving squash and stretch (the physical deformations displayed by an animated figure as modified by imagined gravity and inertia), keeping a template scale version of a character is not a bad idea. In sequence exercises, deliberately exaggerating scale and then drawing in scale can mimic things like squash and stretch.

Drawing the figure in sequence in differing views or perspectives is an additional necessary exercise. Purely profile views are obviously impractical for use all of the time. Much of life and animation involves views moving toward or away from the viewer, sometimes directly and sometimes at differing angles. There are also bird's-eye views and worm's-eye views, and combinations of all of these.

To have dramatic punch and a sense of reality, this knowledge of differing perspectives is invaluable.

figure | 4-15 |

Worm's-eye, bird's-eye, and other points of view.

WALK FIRST, RUN LATER

Artists must become familiar, as animators, of walk and run cycles. This is for both human beings and the various animals, as well. Basic walk and run cycles should be perfected from profile views first, and then in various viewing angles.

Cycles in Animation?

No, we're not talking about Harleys or velocipedes here. An animation cycle is an animated movement that can be constantly repeated over time without adding new frames (images) to the sequence. The last image of a cyclical sequence feeds into the first image in the sequence (i.e., 1-2-3-4-5-6-7-8-9-1-2-3-4-5-6-7-8-9-1-2-3-4…).

The variation between, say, a tall, thin supermodel's walk and Alfred Hitchcock's walk is dramatic, despite the fact that both are human beings. The number of frames in the cycle for a walk can vary because of different speeds, gaits, and levels of realism. However, being able to repeat each portion of the walk from front to back and beginning to end gives the animator a believable motion. The following examples are just a few of the endless types of walks.

figure | 4-16 |

Examples of different types of walk cycles.

However, key parts of them are apparent. Beginning, crossing gait, push off point, and eleva-tion are just some things to learn and apply. Sequence drawings can mimic these cycles, although the model will need some support help in parts of the cycle. Run cycles, which are similar to walk cycles, can really only be learned from stop-action photography and film. Below are a few run sequences to study.

figure | **4-17**

Some examples of run cycles.

Walks and runs that do not occur in a profile view should be carefully scrutinized for the functionality of their perspective and foreshortening. Drawing sequences from the model that resemble walk cycles and doing studies from photo resources are both highly recommended. Some valuable sources are Muybridge and athletic or dance studies done for the Olympic games and other sporting events.

MAKE A FACE!

Facial expression as a sequential activity can be included in this chapter, although it also belongs in characterization, anatomy, and other areas as well. But here it provides a good foothold for looking at and trying out some sequences involving the human face. As touched upon in the chapter on anatomy, the human face is capable of a myriad of "poses" or expressions, and these can move and change rapidly as circumstances change for the character.

As an introduction to expression and its place in sequence, let's look at some varied expressions and how they are produced. The three areas locally affected are the forehead, eye region, and mouth, with the chin as part of the mouth area.

Each of these areas can act alone, to a certain extent, and they can also act in combination. When the eyes are involved, there is a certain added intensity to the emotion. 'The eyes are the seat of the soul', as is often said. There is no doubt that the eyes have great emotional impact. Mammals frequently display their intent through eye expression. It should be noted that birds and reptiles do not have the facial anatomy to produce such expressions and therefore rely heavily on body language and sound to communicate intent.

The forehead is also a great projector of emotion. Some typical movements that portray emotional states are the single raised eyebrow, with one eye slightly more open than the other (doubt or distrust) and the full brow furrow (anger or deep emotion). The mouth is also an instigator of emotional response, by showing the upward retraction of the corners of the mouth (happiness).

figure | 4-18 |

Facial expression.

figure | 4-19 |

Various facial expressions.

From a quiet, bland facial expression to one full of emotion spins a sequence of change, orchestrated by various muscle groups. Sometimes the mouth opens, involving the jaw muscles, and sometimes the eyes open, squeeze shut, or are only slits. Below are some simple facial expression sequences.

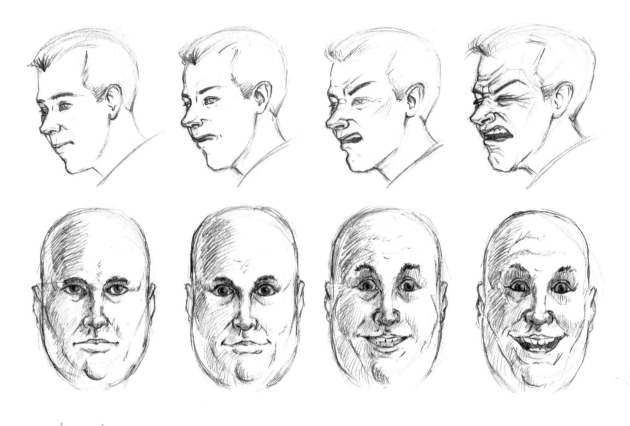

figure | **4-20** |

Facial expression sequences.

In drawn or computer-generated characters, expression of emotion is one of the hardest areas to make convincing, due to the subtle and plastic qualities of facial emotion. Remember: convincing character animation requires real-life observation!

CHAPTER SUMMARY

The importance of sequential drawing from life as a key reference element for 2D animation drawing cannot be stressed enough. The visualization of anatomy in motion over time is paramount to the ability to draw successful animation. A working knowledge of anatomy, perspective, foreshortening, and the way in which gravity affects a moving body in space will all help to define the parameters that are required for translating sequential reference into workable, sequential drawings. Understanding the concepts of cyclical drawing for animation and its interdependence with sequential drawing is crucial to the development of the 2D animator's skill set.

exercises

1. Draw three- and four-step sequences for thirty minutes at a time. Have the model try unusual sequences such as tumbling, rising from supine positions, etc.

2. Draw three- and five-step sequences with alternating steps missing; then fill in the absent steps without the model.

3. Do a sequence that only involves rotating the figure. The model should choose the same repeatable pose and face a different direction for each part of the sequence.

4. Draw only the torso in a sequence; then repeat the poses adding arms, legs, and head.

5. Do sequences, observing and marking points such as shoulders, hip joints, etc.

6. Do sequences and draw in the line of motion.

7. Mark the center of gravity and its changes in some sequences.

8. Draw sequences from models that resemble walk cycles.

9. Using a mirror, draw your own face in various facial expressions. Then try moving your face in incremental steps into these expressions, recording each step. Remember, the face must finally relax after expression.

in review

1. What is the definition of sequence drawing?

2. What is meant by the term center of gravity?

3. What is the definition of the animation cycle? How does sequence drawing apply to creating an animation cycle?

4. How is sequence drawing directly related to key-framing for animation?

MAINTAINING THE CREATIVE MACHINE

michael sickinger

Michael Sickinger, an accomplished Graphic Designer, is Art Director of the Flavors Creative Marketing Studio at Firmenich, a flavor and fragrance company. Michael also frequents colleges and universities, speaking to students about working in the field of graphic design.

Maintaining the creative machine means exactly that—creativity needs constant maintenance to keep running at maximum potential. Creativity must be fed with anything and everything you can get your hands, eyes, and mind on. Tools to keep your thoughts clean and running strong are everywhere, you just need to know how and where to find them.

Having a keen eye is the key to properly maintaining a strong creative mind. A sharp eye will catch all that is around to be seen. Give yourself a new perspective and try to look at things differently. Use your eyes and mind together to see more than just what is there. This not only has you looking for visuals in a more innovative light, but also gives the eyes and mind a good creative workout.

- Keep your eyes peeled when watching television, a movie, or surfing the Web. Paying attention to graphics at your leisure will build your creative toolbox with items that could be needed at a later date. Notice how things are laid out, how they animate, if the font matches the mood, and most of all, think to yourself: how can I do that?

- A finely tuned creative engine is always upgrading to something newer and faster; don't become last year's model! One thing that's good, and bad, about a career in visual communications is that it's constantly evolving. Computers have revolutionized the industry, and change happens almost every day. In order to be competitive, you must stay up to date with technology and learn as much as you can as fast as you can. There are always things to be learned; don't fall behind and let technology pass you by.

- Another important maintenance procedure for creativity is to keep in tune with the design of the times. Just like computers, design changes over time. An ad created in the early '90s probably won't look as cutting edge during the present. Keep those creative gears greased with current design technique and style in order to keep your creativity looking shiny and new.

- As with any mechanical device, there are things that can keep the device from working properly: inhibitors. Creativity works the same way. Having something on your mind while trying to be creative is like a pebble caught in a cog; there's something in the way of it functioning correctly. If you're too busy thinking about what happened yesterday, you're not going to be able to focus on what you have to do today. Take a walk, have some coffee, or listen to a good CD. Clear your head and get those creative spark plugs crackling.

A machine will break down and cease to operate if not maintained on a routine basis. Creativity will do the same. In order to keep creativity fresh and exciting, you must be willing to give it what it needs. Keep your creativity on the cutting edge by constantly feeding it with new visuals, technology, up-to-date design exposure, and stay away from creative inhibitors. Keep these things in mind, and your creativity will be running at maximum potential.

dramatic action and living beings

objectives

Acquire an understanding of different types of action relating to humans and animals

Define and use the line of action

Learn some tips for drawing dramatic action

Grasp the use of *point of view* for describing dramatic action

introduction

How do we define the "dramatics" of drawing for animation? Simply: 2D animation is a medium that is used to tell a story visually. As storytellers, we have a responsibility to the audience to draw stimulating imagery that keeps the viewer's interest. If the moving imagery is boring or poorly done, no one pays attention to the story. On the drawing level, we can break this concept down into figurative dynamics (which includes animal movement), and spatial (or scenic) dynamics.

Figurative dynamics refers to the visual strength of the pose/action in any given drawing or frame of a character/animated sequence. If we think of an animated character sequence or movement as getting from point A to point B, then how we go the distance must be visually interesting. We can also think of extremes (keys) in figurative animation as going from one interesting pose or illustration to the next.

figure | 5-1 |

Two stages of dynamism
in line of action.

figure | 5-2 |

Twisted line of action.

Is the pose of the figure in the drawing visually interesting, or is it boring? Does the drawing have "life"? Does it seem like it could move any
minute? Why? The line of action determines these concepts. If we imagine the main line of action of any given pose as a line passing through the
spine of a figure, any shift of this line away from the center becomes
more dynamic.

The line of action defines the basic movement of the pose.
Shifting weight or twisting/rotating on multiple axes modifies
the line of action and therefore modifies the pose. Straight
and parallel lines are stiff and boring.

figure | 5-3 |

Twisted line of action.

figure | 5-4 |

Diagonal line of action.

Arcs suggest movement. Extremes in the placement of the line of action suggest an off-balance figure, which we equate with motion.

Animation is action. Action can be described in many ways. For example, we can talk about movements being linear or describing an arc like a pendulum (which describes the nature of all movements made by organic beings). Motion can have duration: sluggish or quick. Some activities or single motions are performed very quickly, but are repeated for long periods of time, like the wing beats of a honeybee.

figure | 5-5 |

Lines of action implying rest and movement.

Other activities, like a sloth crawling on a tree branch, have little speed, but last over a long period of time.

Dramatic action, as we have said, is directed toward grabbing and keeping the viewer's attention. All of the above factors and more can influence dramatic action. But the primary thing for the artist/animator to learn is how to utilize these qualities to optimize the effect.

figure | 5-6 |

Fast action: rapid wing beats of the bee.

figure | 5-7 |

Slow action of a sloth.

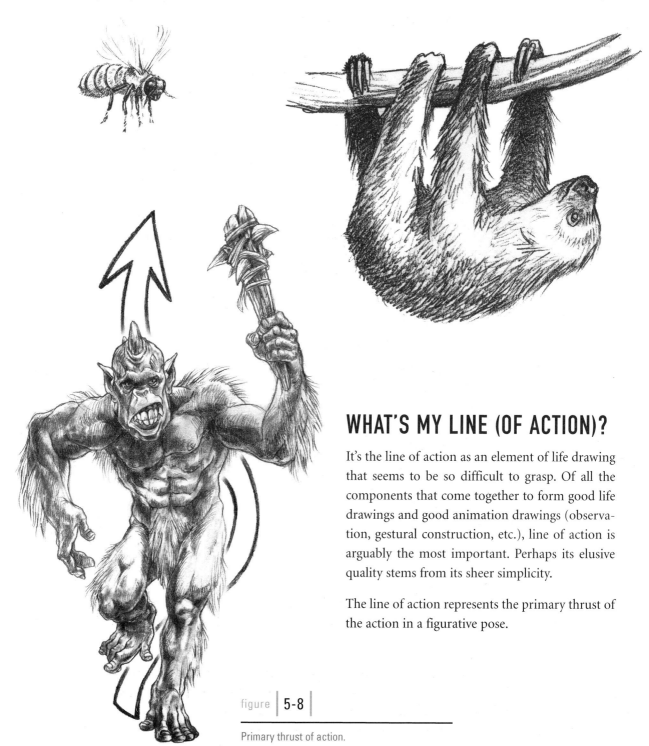

WHAT'S MY LINE (OF ACTION)?

It's the line of action as an element of life drawing that seems to be so difficult to grasp. Of all the components that come together to form good life drawings and good animation drawings (observation, gestural construction, etc.), line of action is arguably the most important. Perhaps its elusive quality stems from its sheer simplicity.

The line of action represents the primary thrust of the action in a figurative pose.

figure | 5-8 |

Primary thrust of action.

Think of drawing one line that would totally describe the movement in a pose. Artists and animators oftentimes become so concerned with the construction of complex technical detail and precise contours that they lose the vivaciousness or gestural quality of the line, not to mention the direction of the pose. This makes for stiff figure and character drawings.

Now, let's look at some different examples of dramatic (and not so dramatic) action. Figure 5-9 shows an invented character in a static pose. Note that an imaginary line of action running through the pose lacks any excitement; it is parallel to the vertical and horizontal lines of the picture plane.

figure | **5-9**

Static line of action.

The line of action is exactly what it implies: the simplest indication, in linear form, of what the character is doing. The action can be dull or still, as in this case, or vigorous and exciting, as in figure 5-10.

Usually, but not always, a dramatic line of action assumes a diagonal thrust (something artists in the Baroque era discovered to be effective), which can also break through the imaginary picture plane. This introduces the problem of foreshortening and whether the artist or director wants the movement to break toward or away from the audience.

figure | 5-10 |

Character in dynamic pose.

A diagonal movement in and of itself doesn't guarantee drama. There are issues of character design, and of squash and stretch, whether the action has torque or rotation, and if the diagonal motion is flexible or stiff, and so on.

A case-by-case review by the artist and director will determine what works best for their specific needs.

What the Heck Is This "Baroque" Era, Anyway?

The Baroque era in art is usually associated with the 17th century in Europe, although its stylistic manifestations appeared as late as the 18th century in some countries. As a "style," the Baroque lent itself to many varied and complex looks. What most predominates is the generation of emotional states and responses through sensuousness, dramatic movement, tension, exotic lighting, and the like. Artists as varied as Rembrandt and Peter Paul Rubens and Guido Reni were part of this movement. So a reference to the dynamic motion, diagonal thrusts in design, and so on, derives from the designs, ceiling paintings, and easel paintings of these masters.

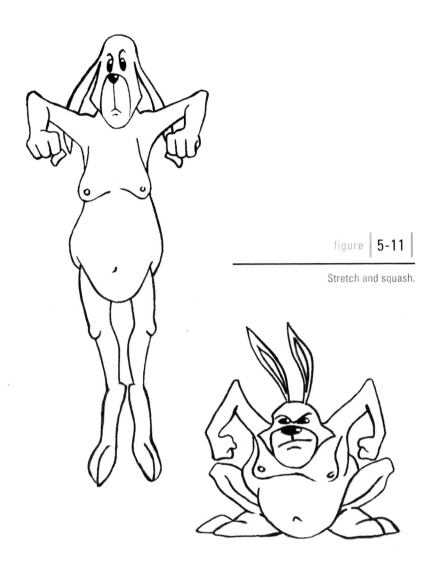

figure | 5-11 |

Stretch and squash.

HUMANS IN MOTION

Human activity covers a wide ground; we often do terribly "undramatic" action most of the time, and it is more commonly in the recreational sports arena or aesthetic realm that drama is seen. Themes that are full of conflict, such as military operations, police action, and so on, frequently use the same basic postures and motion that are displayed in sports, martial arts, or dance.

By using knowledge of human anatomy and pictorial resources, the artist can copy and dramatize (by exaggeration) these motions and poses. Exaggeration in character animation and drawing is paramount. Such overemphasis gives visual clues about the nature of character movement and mood to the audience. Exaggeration means several things. For one, the artist can change or enhance the body itself, as is done with comic book characters. Also, the motion itself that is depicted by a drawn pose can be extended, bent, or diminished for dramatic effect.

figure | 5-12 |

Dramatic pose from martial arts.

figure | 5-13 |

Dramatic pose from dance.

figure | **5-14** |

Exaggeration in a pose.

Typically, the solution uses what we described earlier: diagonal thrust combined with strong drawing and believable characterization.

The distance that a body moves and/or its speed can be enhanced. In more cartoon-like venues, the squash and stretch technique can be added for good measure. *Rotoscoping* (tracing over live-action film for animation) may be a useful tool, but its danger is immediately apparent: the artist is limited by the skill of the physical actors. Even with deliberate modification, activity traced from live reference is more conservative and bound by the nature of its source. Rotoscoping also creates the temptation to forget the skills of life drawing so that if a need for modification arises, the ability may not be available. Nevertheless, the need is real for actual film footage or motion-capture techniques to be used as reference for animation drawing.

HORSES AND CHEETAHS AND ROACHES, OH, MY!

The key to effective figure/character drawing is a working knowledge of human and animal anatomy. Animals (and animal-related characters) present many different problems for the artist. No single book could begin to catalog all the possible animal movements.

Animals make characteristic motions based on anatomy, intent of action, and mood. We might expect an angry, wounded rhinoceros to charge with blind fury, and a playful Dalmatian puppy to yip, run, and gnaw on his master's slipper. What might we expect from the lowly octopus? Sinuous, flowing undulations. Rubbery, lashing tentacles. A speedy departure in a cloud of ink.

figure | **5-15**

Different body types: Mexican wolf.

The animal kingdom contains a huge range of body types, such as wolves, beetles, jellyfish, and snakes. All have different bioengineering plans and therefore different modes of motion. Those more closely related to humans have movements similar in some ways to ours. An animal like a cockroach moves and darts about in a less familiar fashion. Artists need to consult anatomical literature and view actual insects (or movies of the same) in order to understand how they run and turn. Just looking at some body types will easily demonstrate this point.

figure | **5-16**

Different body types: beetle.

figure | 5-17 |

Different body types: jellyfish.

figure | 5-18 |

Different body types: snake.

Let us look at some common animals and their motions. Bipedal animals like humans are really animals that use both two- and four-legged gaits (chimpanzees, etc.). Most animals that have similar bodies to humans still have quite different pelvises, shoulder girdles, and foot designs (see Chapter 3). There are several good photographic/literary sources for animal motion such as Muybridge and Hultgren. Nature documentaries and related films can provide useful images, as can stock photography. Just remember to respect copyright laws at all times!

These animals use some form of *digitigrade* (walking on toes) motion, while bears (and humans) use *plantigrade* (flat-footed) motion. This changes the leg configuration considerably. The range of possible motion of living creatures is directly affected by their respective physical structures. We expect bears and apes to rely predominantly on quadrupedal locomotion, but we also know that the anatomical structure of their pelvic girdles and lower limb musculature allows them to stand up on their hind legs and walk for short periods of time. Some types of movement are intrinsic to certain groups of animals. Carnivores stalk, leap/pounce, grab, bite, and shake their prey from side to side.

THE ANIMATOR
AT WORK

Max Fleischer

Born in Vienna, Max Fleischer (1883–1972) moved with his family to New York City early in his life. Like other animation figures, he showed early promise as an artist, and began his career by studying at the famous Art Students League and Cooper Union in New York, where he honed his technique. From this beginning he worked both as a cartoonist and a commercial artist, but was naturally inquisitive and interested in mechanics. This interest led him to try his hand at animation.

He opened his own animation studio and began producing animated films of various lengths.

Technical invention and creative ideas were part of Fleischer's legacy to the animation industry. He was the most important member of the New York style of animation, where the drawn, non-naturalistic style was most important. Among his staff were strong representations of the Jewish and Italian populations of New York, and this influenced many of his productions. With his brothers Joseph and David, he invented the technique of rotoscoping, a process where live-action film was used as a template, and then animators traced over the live, moving figures to produce the action animation. The first example of this was seen in the film *Experiment Number 1* (1915). This technique was used extensively in a later, full-length feature film *Gulliver's Travels*. Fleischer's studio produced the first sound cartoons, utilizing the DeForest Phonofilm process.

One of his animators, the remarkable Grim Natwick (born Myron Nordveig in Norway), created the famous character Betty Boop, which was one of the more lucrative characters in the Fleischer stable. Unfortunately, Grim received nothing for this creation, and to his dying day was somewhat bitter about this treatment by Fleischer. Natwick went on to work for Walt Disney Studios, being one of the older animators there. His work on *Snow White and the Seven Dwarfs* (especially Snow White herself) was crucial to its success.

Max Fleischer died in Woodland Hills, California, in 1972.

| NOTE |

Generally speaking, students in public college settings are allowed to use copyrighted material for assignments as long as it is only for in-class work. Copyrighted material may not be used outside the classroom for promotion or sale. Students in proprietary schools may not use such copyrighted images, as these schools are for profit, and do not fall under the *fair use* interpretation of the law. When you are creating imagery, remember this general rule of thumb: your final product must be substantively different enough from any sources you used or imitated that an impartial judge would not conclude that your work is a copy. That means being creative; take care with your products so that you do not put yourself in the path of litigation. Your own works are de facto copyrighted as you produce them, but you may want to date and mail a copy to yourself to prove that you actually were the agent of their production.

figure | **5-19** through **5-22** |

Examples of a horse, cat, dog, and an elephant.

If you've ever tickled your pet tabby's tummy, you know how easily she can wrap her paws around your forearm and playfully bite. Feline forelegs are designed to grab and hold their prey while they wrestle it to the ground, i.e., a lion bringing down a zebra. As an artist, you need to understand animal movement in order to replicate it in animation. This information is also critical in the construction of imaginary or extinct creatures with design and movement that are based on known animal anatomy. Some examples might be a dragon after a lizard, or a unicorn after a horse.

In constructing dramatic animal poses for use in animation, we must also take into consideration the intended action and mood. Here's an example: We are required to create an animated sequence of a saber-toothed tiger leaping from a rocky precipice. Is it pouncing onto the back of an unwary mammoth, or playfully leaping into the midst of some wrestling cubs? Is the animal snarling, tense, and displaying machine-like precision, or tongue-lolling, tail-lashing frolic? The action is a pounce. The mood: menacing or benign?

Think about the kinds of movements an animal can make and dramatize them.

figure | 5-23

Lizard image used to produce
dragon character.

STEALING THE SCENE

Animation is a story told through moving sequential art, illustrated with characters and environments. The character animation is dependent on its environment and how it interacts with that environment to produce a story. Scenic dynamics refer to the creative composition of character and background in animation. Backgrounds and characters must combine to form a good visual composition. The script and storyboard outline these issues.

Scenic design in animation is shot-specific. Animation is cinema, so we deal with camera shots in relationship to the viewer. As the camera (view of the character) moves, the perspective and the portion of the scene being viewed change.

Although much action takes place at normal eye level for an average person, considerable live and animated action in movies happens at more unusual eye levels (worm's-eye or bird's-eye views). A virtual camera with the lens parallel to the ground and perpendicular to the subject produces an uninteresting view. Raise or lower the camera. Move it around, above or under the subject. Zoom in or zoom out. Different camera angles create different effects. In a

figure | 5-24 |

Dragon character derived from a lizard image.

worm's-eye view, for instance, a character looks large and imposing with great foreshortening. Some examples are shown in figures 5-25 and 5-26.

It becomes apparent that strong drawing skills are tremendously important for the artist when dealing with storyboards, character design, and animation. Even if the final result is computer-generated imagery, remember that even in these points of view the artist and director must consider whether the character comes directly toward the viewer or moves in a partial diagonal, even though the action can be very foreshortened.

Dynamic layout for a scene in animation includes two important points: choosing visually interesting camera shots to present the action, and creating a composition that gives space for character action to occur. Both of these elements should complement the story that's being told.

figure | 5-25 |

"Bird's eye" point of view.

figure | 5-26 |

"Worm's eye" point of view.

Remember, this is a very visual (and visceral) kind of art. To provoke feeling in the audience requires a lot of preliminary sketching and experimenting with different visual options. As with all art, although the artist may be in love with the product, it is ultimately up to the consumer to be the final judge. Don't keep a product if it does not fulfill the needs of your project. Go back to the proverbial drawing board (but do save the first version for yourself) and try again; your drawing practice will come through in the end.

figure | 5-27 |

Extremely foreshortened
(bird's-eye view) character.

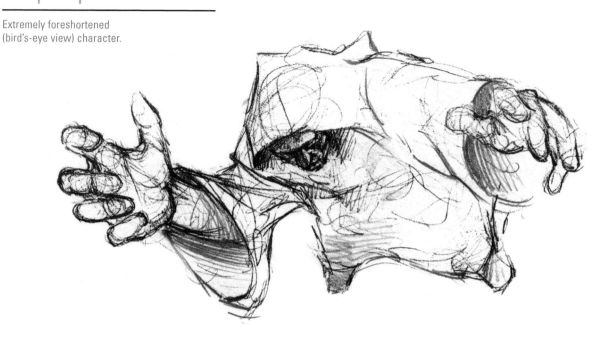

CHAPTER SUMMARY

Dynamism as a key element in portraying action and movement in animation is paramount to the animation artist. Solid drawing ability, good observation skills, and an understanding of foreshortening allow the animation artist to successfully draw human and animal forms in exaggerated poses. Visualizing the figure and scenic elements from different angles is important for creating shot-specific views in animation design.

exercises

1. Working from the live model, practice drawing a series of static poses, followed by a series of action poses.

2. Using the drawings from the first exercise, create tracing paper overlays for each drawing on which you've indicated the line of action. Compare.

3. Using figure drawings done from a live model, redraw the images with exaggerated poses and anatomy. Be aware of changes in perspective and foreshortening.

4. Utilizing photographic or other life-drawing resources, create a series of gesture drawings with dominant lines of action as practice in defining dramatic poses.

5. Utilizing photographic or other life-drawing resources, draw a human figure or animal as seen from several different points of view to explore how the dramatic possibilities of the pose increase or decrease by virtue of those changes.

in review

1. How is exaggeration used in 2D animation?

2. How does point-of-view affect the dynamics of a pose?

3. How does the line of action affect the dynamics of a pose?

4. What three factors can affect the characteristic movements of animals (or humans)?

animation architecture

objectives

introduction

What is animation without a background? It's a costume drama on an empty stage. *Scenery and background structure are storytelling elements that set up the following factors in an animated scene: environment, staging, mood, context, and scale.*

Because of the nature of the animation background, it also seems to be a very mysterious, if not forgotten, piece of the artistic puzzle to budding animators. Many artists and animators enjoy drawing figures and characters, but not architecture and backgrounds. By the same token, other artists find that they are more attracted to constructing a village or a mountain scene than in evolving the stories of heroes and villains. The skills learned in the life-drawing classroom relate just as much to these images as to humans and animals. Proportional measuring, use of line, and so forth don't change just because the subject is a Mayan temple. Whether drawing an oil lamp or the Taj Mahal, consistent use of these principles will make or break the success of the rendering.

However, the reluctance of many to approach the drawing of scenic elements perhaps has something to do with that vile beast which rears its ugly head at the mention of illustrated scenery: *perspective!*

ANIMATION ARCHITECTURE

VANISHING POINT: GOING, GOING, GONE...

Let's do a brief visual recap of perspective and its definition.

Perspective systems typically attempt to mimic how the human eye perceives the world around it. Fish-eye lens effects, binocular vision, and other issues are not dealt with; in fact, they are ignored. The systems used are, as a result, limited imitations of vision.

Several limiting factors in drawing perspective should be noted. First, *the apparent eye level of the viewer/artist limits the type of view and correspondent placement of parts of the perspective system.* Although we normally view the environment at standing or seated levels, other types of view occur frequently. Lying on the front lawn and looking upwards at a family member can radically alter your point of view; equally, staring over the edge of a cliff can render your normal perspective haywire.

The point at which the viewer is situated in plain view is called the *station point,* and only occurs in a diagram from a top (bird's-eye) view. It is used when establishing a diagram for constructing, say, a building for an architectural rendering. This allows other elements and ideal viewpoints to be explored in relation to the viewer. Normal eye level is between five and six feet, diagrammatically, and will always correspond to the apparent horizon line, where sky and earth meet (without intervening objects) for a viewer who is standing vertically on the earth "plane." In perspective, we deal with this ground as though it were flat, not curved, to avoid unnecessary technical entanglements. The *horizon line* is abbreviated HL, and *station point* is SP.

Once an eye level has been chosen, the objects to be drawn and their environment become limited by this position. Tall objects or structures may overlap the horizon line above and below. It will immediately become obvious that some objects are seen "corner on," that is, they are not parallel to the picture plane. Other objects may be parallel to the picture plane. In fact, only objects that contain parallel lines in their vertices are easy to construct in perspective, due to their simplicity.

As real objects recede in space from the observer, their frontal regions appear larger, relative to the receding portions, due to foreshortening. If it is a simple object—for example, a shipping box—the vertices that are parallel appear to converge as it recedes; in fact, if the lines were continued, they would appear to meet at a point on the horizon line (if they are parallel to the ground). This is called a *vanishing point* (or VP). When looking at a simple geometric object in the center of the field of view that is parallel to the picture plane, we get what is known as *one-point perspective.* This one point refers to the single dominant vanishing point. One-point perspective is useful in limited shots that involve straight-on views, where the peripheral parts of the scene are less important than the center action. At the edge of all one-point perspective is a built-in distortion that gets worse the farther you travel from center. Usually artists fudge the outer portions of these designs to minimize the diagonal pull on the forms as they get farther from the center vanishing point region. It is very useful in focusing the viewer on a smaller visual region, and is less complex to construct.

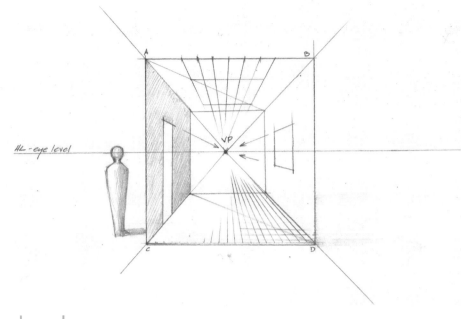

figure | **6-1a**

One-point perspective.

The name, as we said, denotes the fact that all parallel surfaces converge on the one vanishing point. But, as the viewer moves away from center, a distortion soon creeps into the drawing, which is due to the fact that in reality, as we move away from center, we are actually in two-point perspective. Two-point perspective refers to a view of objects that are not parallel to the observer's picture plane, but are, instead, seen as turned toward the viewer, giving more than one surface to look at—and thus two vanishing points.

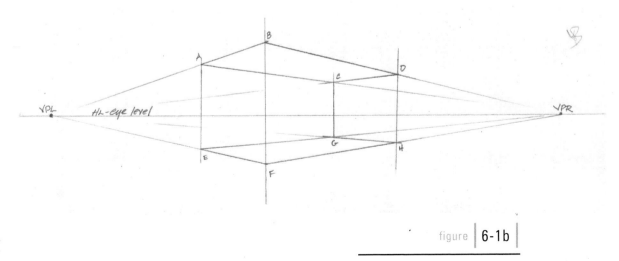

figure | **6-1b**

Two-point perspective.

figure | 6-1c |

Three-point perspective.

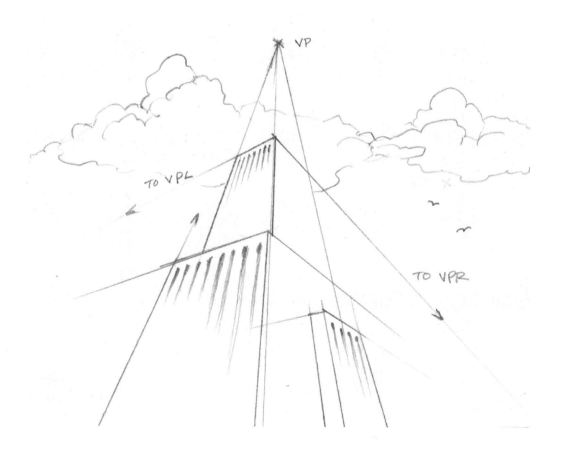

Convergence still holds sway, but now we must account for more than one surface. Clearly, this system and one-point perspective systems are easiest to understand when working with simple solids.

As the viewpoint becomes lower or higher, convergence becomes more apparent in vertical directions, and a third vanishing point must be established to construct these objects. This is three-point perspective. In actuality, all perspective systems are three-point systems; by convention, we tend to ignore the small changes in scale when doing small areas in a rendering.

Further explanation of perspective, including shadows, reflections, ellipses, and so on, are covered in texts dealing only with perspective. What you will find useful to remember is that if you can construct a three-dimensional grid governed by the vanishing points and the horizon line, and then place simple solids on it, converting the simpler forms to more complex ones (that must basically fit the space), then using vanishing points and scale on the grid itself, take these forms and the surrounding area and produce a final design/drawing. At this point, it is advised that you go to texts dealing with reflections and shadows and other special cases if you have problems developing your image. The truth is that most background artists now make guestimations, based upon their basic knowledge of perspective, or utilize computer programs that can provide the basic context from which to overlay drawn elements.

Another thing to consider is atmospheric perspective, where the intervening dust and air scatter and absorb light so that the more distant objects become fainter and (if you are using color) bluer. Another element is textural perspective, where cues of constantly diminishing patterns (such as the bricks on a building) give the viewer the sense of space. Using overlap, scale, and cues from the objects themselves, an authentic spatial relationship can be constructed and then elaborated upon. Top view diagrams (with the viewer inserted as the station point) give the artist the means to actually build a building from the ground up, using elevations and ground plan as guides (sides and top view). This methodology still requires the basic vanishing points and straight edges to achieve its ends, and a good freehand artist can simulate this method quite surprisingly well. Vanishing points, horizon line (eye level), and a simple scale are basically all that's needed to produce a good perspective drawing.

SITE SEEN OR UNSEEN

The process of creating scenic elements for animation requires direct, observational reference drawn from life. Sketching these elements from life can be a daunting task for the beginning animator/background artist. It will be fairly obvious now that the principles given earlier about drawing in general will relate as well to drawing architectural elements, landscapes, and other non-character subjects. The basic underlying structure for architectural sketching is the quick sketch, or gesture, drawing. *The keys to creating effective gesture drawings of architectural elements are a basic understanding of the rules of perspective, preplanning your vantage point(s) to maximize the potential use of the sketches, and the use of proportional measuring.*

| NOTE |

Call Them (ad)Vantage Points!

Backgrounds for animation are shot-specific, meaning that they are designed from a specific vantage point that establishes the camera angle and even the apparent depth-of-field of each given shot in an animated film.

Considering architectural drawings, there are some issues that come first when constructing a rendering. The eye level and the distance from the building(s) or object(s) need to be chosen first. The artist will have given thought to the type and style of structure to be drawn, and then, after researching the details of the architectural style both historically and technically, thumbnails should be drawn, showing both the type of buildings to be rendered and their general layout or compositional sense.

These thumbnails are crucial to developing the final product, because this is where ideas that don't work, inappropriate eye levels, scale considerations, and so forth can be resolved.

figure | 6-2 |

Scenic thumbnails.

| NOTE |

We're Talkin' Old School

Many neighborhoods sport interesting or antique architecture that make for excellent drawing resources for animation backgrounds. Some towns and cities may have substantial Victorian architecture, while others are located near the ruins of Native American pueblos. Search your hometown for interesting architecture and your region for other exciting scenic features such as mountains, deserts, and seashores. You might find many local background design elements that are useful for observational reference.

Both architecture and the human figure can be confusing to the viewer until the underlying forms and structure of these objects is understood. It is useful to reduce the complex human figure to its base form for structural reference, as seen in the guise of the drawing manikin. Drawing environments should be approached in the same manner as one would approach figure drawing: create an initial sketch of the simple volumetric forms to establish volumes, and then refine/detail after you make sure the gesture drawing works. Remember: work simple to complex or big to small. Work roughly and try to capture the character of the scenery rather than its minutiae; that's what photographs are for!

Stephen Missal

The creation of flora and fauna in "native" environments provides visual support for story development

Creative creature invention is a great animation brainstorming tool

Background design and its relation
to character movement is paramount
to animation layout

Stephen Missal

Important storytelling
elements such as
special visual effects
can be effectively
planned through
production illustration

Stephen Missal

Human/animal hybrids are a
classical character form and
provide the basic concept
behind many animation characters and other invented beings

Stephen Missal

Human and animal forms present important reference material for extrapolating imaginary creatures

Stephen Missal

Exploration of character variation and attitude is a key element in a character design

Kevin Hedgpeth

Color use in figure drawing is a valuable skill
element for the animator artist and designer

Terrance Yee

Stephen Missal

Stephen Missal

Good composition blends scenic elements and character action
in a way that advances visual storytelling

Kevin Hedgpeth

Kevin Hedgpeth

Doodles and thumbnail drawings act as an idea springboard
for creating related visuals for story concepts and layout

Kevin Hedgpeth

Digital coloring and image processing is an
important aspect of animation design. A strong
drawing ability enhances this skill set

Kevin Hedgpeth

Stephen Missal

Stephen Missal

Lighting design through story illustration is a factor in layout

Kevin Hedgpeth

**The addition of color and some extra anatomical elements to a figure drawing
can create new character designs**

Kevin Hedgpeth

Colored pencil is a fun and effective medium for creating life drawings

Kevin Hedgpeth

Drawing the human figure in unique poses with foreshortening helps the animation artist to develop a feel for character movement in space

Stephen Missal

Interiors with characters in unusual combinations can produce unexpected drama and moods

Stephen Missal

figure | 6-3 |

Architectural gesture.

Buildings and other scenic elements can typically be reduced to a grouping of simple geometric solids (cubes, cylinders, and spheres), placed in perspective, and then more fully rendered into an image that actually looks like the real thing. The reverse is also true. We can describe a series of simple solids in perspective and then make them look like a clump of trees, antediluvian ruins of eons past, or a Spanish mission.

MOOD AND MOONLIGHTING

Lighting is an important aspect of background design. It is a primary contributing factor toward the look of a scene and directly affects characters and other elements of animated action. Illumination, mood, and focus are the key operations of lighting in an animated scene, and we will discuss them as they apply to drawing for creative storytelling in animation.

| NOTE |

Just Putting Things in Perspective

A good working knowledge of perspective rules is helpful when properly breaking them. Practice creating technical perspective drawings, but keep this in mind: when sketching an environment, don't whip out a T-square and a calculator to triangulate vanishing points—just eyeball it! Artists who have a strong understanding of perspective often just fake it. If the drawing appears believable to the audience, it works.

figure | 6-4 |

Working from simple solids to more
detailed drawings in architecture.

One of the main uses of lighting in an animated scene is to make the important scenic elements more visible. In other words, we're throwing light on the scene so we can see what's
going on, action-wise.

Typically, outdoor locations are going to be illuminated only by natural lighting (sunlight or
moonlight), but may also be affected by other light sources like fire, street lamps, or reflected
interior lighting (in the case of buildings).

Observation of real-world lighting conditions allows the artist to visualize the properties of
lighting in an animated scene. Lighting has to be logically devised so that the audience will
believe in its effects. The moon will illuminate a character from above while a campfire

figure | 6-5 |

Lighting in architectural and scenic drawings.

bathes him\her in low-angle lighting. To this end, observe and sketch scenic elements at various times of the day and night to see how light affects objects and scenes. You'll note that sketching lighting effects with value (grayscale) is imperative so as to depict shadow areas with a sense of realism.

Creating a specific mood for a background is most important in the creation of good scenic context and storytelling. Mood refers to an *implied feeling* that is conjured for the audience by the visual nature of the scene, aided by sound, lighting, structure, and action. Lighting is a major player in this scenario. The predominance and quality of lighting directly affect the mood of the scene. Deep, dark shadows can suggest drama, gloominess, and mystery.

figure | **6-6** |

Use of light and shadow in scenic drawings as dramatic reinforcement.

Shadows are useful for obscuring elements of the scene that are unimportant or not meant to be seen by the audience. This concept is useful in horror films for cloaking the beastie prepared to spring onto the unwary protagonist from the darkness.

Bright, high-key lighting can help to create a cheerful, sunny day in the park or muster the warm illumination of Santa's workshop. Minimized contrast with intense omni-directional lighting reduces the dramatic aspects of a scene and therefore lends itself to becoming a background aspect for comedy and lighter subjects. Minimal contrast in lighting does not necessarily suggest a happy scene: a cloudy and gloomy winter's day will usually have low-contrast, diffuse lighting of a relatively strong nature. Winter lighting may also owe itself to a reflective blanket of snow-covered terra firma.

Note that reflective light illuminates animated characters as well as the primary light source does.

Focus, as the subject refers to scenic lighting, is not an element of cinematographic optics, but the manner in which lighting determines the amount of viewing importance relegated to any background element, animated object, or character, relative to the audience. *In the most basic compositional sense, focus means literally spotlighting the background or animation to grab the viewer's attention.* Here's an example of focus: imagine peering down the vaulted hallway of an ancient catacombs or dungeon, viewing an opposite tunnel lit only by a singular, unknown light source. Two half-silhouetted figures run across the lit stone floor of your path ahead. Focused lighting, as per our example, plays a role in blocking the character action in a scene.

The light source must illuminate an unobstructed section of the dungeon tunnel in order to allow the viewer to see the running characters. This use of lighting directly affects storytelling. If the audience

figure | 6-7 |

Reflected light used in scenic drawing.

figure | 6-8 |

Focused lighting for drama in a scenic drawing.

loses interest or has its attention diverted due to bad lighting (or any other misused visual element), the story fails.

There are clear factors in deciding how to construct a background or setting for the characters. Among our determined criteria are scale, that is, at what scale to represent the setting in relation to the character(s); lighting, which to a great extent gives us how visible the scene and characters are, and in what mood the piece is to be viewed; natural setting, or what actual context in nature is to be used (if at all); and style, as in Victorian architecture versus Gothic, or some fantasy hybrid of architectural elements.

figure | 6-9

Architectural fantasies.

To integrate the characters into a context requires a unity of stylistic treatment, first of all, and to this end we again emphasize how important it is to research that information. Costume, hairstyles, even manner of walking can be culture-specific, and will seem out of place in the wrong context. We also visually manipulate the scene to promote the highest level of interest or to correctly tell the story. To do this may mean choosing a particular point of view, or that plus a certain scale for the character(s) within that camera shot. A close-up of a face with a hint of a towering edifice behind it gives a very different feel from a mid-shot, eye-level view of the same character at the base of the same structure.

One is hyper-dramatic, the other rather tame. Obscuring the view with useless detail or extra material can ruin a shot.

figure | 6-10 |

Contrasting views of the same scene
with differing scales.

Lighting that does not allow the same information can also hinder the storytelling. On the other hand, plain, omni-directional lighting such as we encounter indoors in a work environment can be so dull that a little creativity on the part of the art director is in order.

Point of view, the simulating of a viewer's angle of view in a shot, leads us to sometimes try several different views for the same scene, to see which works the best. Now we are back to the gestural type of drawing from our earlier chapters. This leads to storyboarding, the art of telling the story of the animation through a sequence of still, loosely drawn pictures showing chronological camera shots. These are used by the director to explore various visual possibilities for each

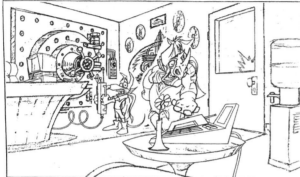

figure | 6-11 |

Storyboard with architectural elements.

scene before committing them to film or digital medium. This is an art in itself, because it combines character drawing, scenic drawing, perspective, lighting, and knowledge of various camera possibilities.

Background sketches play an important, if supportive role in storyboards. They must reinforce the story without becoming the subject themselves. A grandiose environment can still work if it is handled simply, and viewed such that the action is clear and understandable. Many Japanese animations have elaborate backgrounds, beautifully painted and very conducive to the storytelling. The trick is to put in just enough information so that the eye believes it is seeing more.

ENTER (OR EXIT) STAGE LEFT!

In an animated scene, as in live action, a character must have the room to move and interact as directed by the script, storyboard, and director. The scene must be capable of allowing the figures (or vehicles or whatever) to maneuver, and to give the viewer a clear idea of what is going on.

In cinema, actors conform to *blocking* or predetermined movement within a scene. The set designer would not place a table in the path of an actor/actress who needs to run through an unobstructed hallway in a given scene. Nor would a layout artist draw a large statue or

Sherman tank in front of a doorway into which an animated character requires easy egress. It is the task of the layout artist to take concept art and storyboard information (where the camera angles have been designed for each scene) and create functional value drawings of each background that will eventually be converted into background paintings.

Simply put, scene layout must not interfere with animated character blocking. Animation backgrounds are designed to give characters *acting space* and must allow the animated action that is part of a scene to function. Here is an example of background layout with proposed character placement.

figure | **6-12** |

Background layout with character overlay.

IN (NOT OUT OF) CONTEXT

Beyond blocking and staging, the animation director and storyboard artist must also consider the creation of a dynamic composition of scenic elements and the placement of character action within the scene.

figure | 6-13 |

Scenery with and without dynamic placement of characters.

This is *framing the action.* Many design and motion issues must be taken into account, including screen direction (which way the action in a scene moves relative to the viewer), and the relation of positive/negative space in the frame. The principal use of scenic drawing for 2D animation is to create an environmental context for character staging. In other words, the animation background sets the stage for character activity. We say background, but we are referring to a camera view of the scene, which will likely incorporate both foreground and background elements.

The Rule of Thirds

Those art-lovin' ancient Greeks have done it again! While searching for ultimate proportion in art and life, the Greek mathematician, Euclid, came up with a divine mathematical ratio, which provided the Greeks with the proportional scale that drove their sense of design. Based on this ratio, the Greeks designed what they considered to be a rectangle with proportions that were thought to be the most pleasing to the eye. This became the Golden Rectangle, whose ratio of height to width is close to the 4:3 aspect ratio of the standard frame of 35mm motion picture film. Even the authors were impressed.

The wonderful *Rule of Thirds,* based on the idea of the Golden Rectangle, says that if we divide the picture plane (the frame or viewable area of the scene) into thirds, both horizontally and vertically, the principle areas of interest in that scene will occur at the intersections of those divisions (marked with dots in figure 6-14).

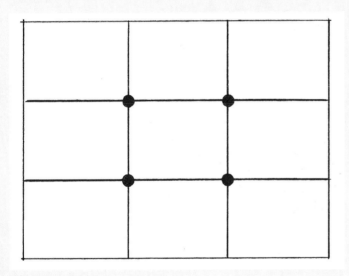

figure | **6-14**

Diagram of the rule of thirds.

Isolated or associated scenic elements can create the idea of an environment without being part of a fully rendered backdrop. Minimal set decoration can oftentimes be as powerful as (or more appropriate than) meticulously painted trompe l'oeil (fool-the-eye real) scenery. For instance, interesting sea plants and coral plus the encrusted remnant of a ship's wooden prow can suggest the environs of a long-forgotten wreck of a Spanish galleon.

A timeworn, bestial idol and a group of leafy fronds can create a "lost world" kind of atmosphere.

figure | 6-15 |

Suggestion in scenic development.

| NOTE |

A Quick, Yet Poignant Reminder!

Avoid scenic clutter that inter-feres with animated action in a scene. Ask yourself these important background design questions: does the scale of the natural element fit the action and the characters? (Improper scale can make a story either indecipherable or laughable.) How's my point of view? (Point of view can also alter how the elements are used.)

figure | 6-16 |

Implied "lost world."

GREENERY

When designing backgrounds, natural objects become an important part of many solutions. Trees, forests, caverns, rivers, and mountains crowd much animation. With the introduction of fractals, some innovative solutions to creating these items became easier for the computer technician. However, in both 2D and 3D animation, hand-generated imagery is both possible and vital in current art solutions. Because of the way in which computer-generated natural objects evolve, it is still necessary—and always will be—to involve the artist in composing, editing, and adding to the product.

Many settings contain trees, bushes, and similar vegetative growth. When drawing these, *remember that all things can (and should) be recorded first in a gestural form.* As a gesture is basically a combination of pose and general physical attributes displayed in quick linear terms, we can readily see that to draw, for example, an oak tree, would emphasize its thick trunk and large branchings from this central axis through a series of massings and strong lines similar to figure 6-17.

figure | 6-17 |

Oak tree sketches in gestural and more developed form.

Detail added to a
preliminary sketch.

After drawing trees and large bushes for some time, one notices that the branches often are staggered in origination from the central stem or trunk. On a pine tree, the sheer verticality of the form overshadows this, but if the branches emerge always at the same level, then a kind of phony artificiality emerges. This is very obvious in trees such as oaks and apples, where the sheer scale of the lower branches makes symmetry obviously wrong. The sequential change in scale from large to small really holds true on trunks, stems, and branches. Reversing the shrinking at the end of a branch gives a kind of goofy Popeye look to it; the tapering has been lost. Another detail that is often lost on the beginner is a kind of angularity that happens as the branches emerge from the center; novices often "rubberize" them by introducing too many gentle curves. One very nice thing about drawing things like trees is that errors are far more forgiving than in drawing people or animals; the variation in branches and similar visual parts is far more encompassing in the vegetable kingdom. We would not do so well with extra arms and misplaced heads or legs.

The leafy areas of most deciduous trees clump or group in fairly discrete areas, allowing the artist to record them more as a mass that individually—much as we record hair. Instead of each leaf being carefully analyzed as an individual form, we learn to apply dark/light textures and symbols to stand for leaves. In fact, most of what we do regarding this part of vegetation involves finding an apt textural stand-in or symbol for the large masses of leaves, smaller branches, and needles. Only later do we add enough (and *only* enough) detail to flesh out these groups into textures readable as leaves of a specific kind or with enough direct information as is necessary in the circumstances.

A group or copse of trees also gets the same treatment; that is, the whole group is treated as a unit (or several large sub-units), with major directional thrusts and massings emphasized first, before breaking this into smaller and smaller levels of detail, just as we did with a single tree. The method remains the same. It also allows us to draw whole scenes more quickly, because we are concentrating on areas in combination rather than accumulating small details into a picture.

Gesture drawing of a stand of trees.

figure | **6-20** |

Evergreens and their
dominant verticality.

Evergreen trees give a slightly different problem, because of the verticality of their growth. The attention will be on the profile of the grouped trees, as much as anything else; these can be overlapped and truncated to meet the needs of the project.

As detail is added to evergreens (including bushy outgrowths), smaller light/dark massings, horizontally layered, will give the impression of the greenery as it relates to the branching.

figure | **6-21** |

Gesture drawing of a stand
of evergreens.

Trees with little or no leaves or needles are both easier and harder to draw, because on the one hand the obscuring greenery is gone, but on the other hand another level of detail and structure becomes more important. Some examples of types of trees that one might encounter in both modes (bare and green) are shown in figure 6-22.

figure | **6-22** |

Variations in tree shapes.

figure | 6-23 |

Buildings (ruins) enhanced by encroaching vegetation.

It should be noted that different types of trees make different branchings and have quite different configurations, even with the commonalities of "tree-dom." Placing the wrong type of vegetation in a scene (a palm tree in an arctic tundra, for example) can truly ruin the mood of a piece. Research is essential in all cases. Smaller undergrowth follows the same rules, with the observation that greenery dominates branches. Buildings can be enhanced by well-placed greenery, or they can be obscured.

Hi-tech scenes obviously tend to ignore natural surroundings, sometimes to their tedium, since the relief from straight lines and glossy surfaces with added greenery (or rock formations) can make the whole scene feel more complete and interesting.

figure | 6-24 |

Futuristic scene.

Exotic greenery, like palms and cycads, still follows the same visual rules given in earlier chapters and reiterated here. Big stuff first, small stuff last. Palms can be slender and tall, or squat and relatively short. All the elements of basic drawing still apply. The most important thing is observation and research, along with strong preliminary drawings. The final renderings can be faithful to a much greater degree of detail, but won't be effective if the overall design is weak, or the scale or kind of vegetation is wrong.

Vegetation can be used to create dynamic design solutions in scenes where drama is indicated. Fantasy situations and similar thematic material often are enhanced by the selective use of silhouetting or enclosure from trees and other greenery. The same concept applies to caves and other rock formations.

figure | 6-25 |

Silhouetting in scenic design.

Drawing scenes from life, where these kinds of devices are actually encountered, can help teach the artist how to invent necessary backgrounds, just as life drawing helps in character animation. *What is true in other art venues applies here: use as much information as you need and then stop. Overuse of detail robs all drama from a scene because the viewer is too busy trying to sort out the small information instead of following the action.* In the case of vegetation, any architectural elements usually depend upon the greenery as a foil, not as a visual mask. In jungle ruins, obviously, this might not be true; however, the overall large forms such as mounds and groupings of plants and architectural elements still dominate.

figure | 6-26 |

Scenery as a foil to man-made forms.

Flat areas and gentle rolling hills follow the general rules of perspective, normally being filled with other, more important plot items such as buildings, characters, space ships, etc. As scenic devices, they mostly add a sense of mood for the action. In urban areas, open spaces have their own psychological impact, because we usually associate those places with more crowded conditions. Thus, a housing project with a field adjacent to it gives us both the sense of city and loneliness at the same time. By the same token, a rural setting with a sudden cluster of buildings or other structures can give a sudden jolt to the peaceful sense of nature without man. These do not need any particular structural study, other than general sketching practice, because they do not contain any complexity that begs further investigation. Other natural structures such as mountains, cliffs, foothills, rock outcroppings, and the like, do invite more involved study. When studying mountains, it is readily apparent that they come in a great variety of sizes and shapes. A mountain may be a jagged, snow- and ice-encrusted "tooth" thrusting skyward, like the Matterhorn, or a gentler cone-shaped affair, such as Mt. Jefferson in the New Hampshire White Mountains. Quite frankly, mountains, volcanoes, and other large-scale rock formations require quite a lot of research. The ways in which they form and erode, along with their age and geographic location, can show considerable variety in the forms the artist may encounter. Some general guiding principles that we have encountered before will help us now. Remember that, as in all drawing from life or life sources, the larger elements are simply observed first, with attention to larger massing and light/dark areas before any attention to detail is undertaken. A gesture of a tree line or a mountain ridge is just as practical as the gesture of a running superhero. After laying in the major information, the artist can then begin resolving finer and finer levels of detail, stopping when the information begins to overwhelm the scene.

ROCKERY

Wind, rain, and similar agents eventually wear the peaks down, so that once magnificent mountain ranges become gentle, softly rounded ones like the Appalachians in the eastern United States. On some ranges, trees soften the appearance of the slopes, giving a kind of hybrid appearance, both alive and green and at the same time harsh and craggy. So the artist must look for layering, direction of large masses, eroded areas that give rise to ridges and valleys, and so on. Smaller rock formations have many of these characteristics on a lesser scale. It is important to have some idea of what sort of rock you are drawing. Sandstone, a sedimentary rock, is softer, and erodes into fantastic shapes and layers. Granite, a granular igneous rock, can form huge batholiths, or masses of rock protruding into other older rocks. Marble is a metamorphic rock, in this case originally sedimentary (deposited grains of eroded rock), that has been transformed underground by

| NOTE |

Mountains can be isolated or in groups or ranges numbering many massifs. They typically are built in several ways. Some are formed by molten lava forcing its way to the surface of the earth, with resultant volcanoes. These can be tall, cone-like affairs such as Mt. Fuji in Japan, or broad, low shield volcanoes, as in Hawaii. They build over time by accretion of material from inside the earth. Their shape is determined by this mechanism. Other mountains form when large blocks of the earth rise, relative to their surroundings; these are fault-block mountains, such as are found in Nevada and Utah. The Black Hills of South Dakota are domes formed by underlying igneous (lava derived) rock. Larger mountain ranges are folded or combinations of folding, faults, and volcanism. Large marine sediment deposits accumulate, later to be shoved upward in these mountain masses by the movements of large tectonic plates that cover the surface of the earth, colliding and brushing against one another in slow but titanic interactions. The sedimentary rocks are layered, and this layering often shows in the upper reaches of mountains as erosion wears away the rock formations. Fault-block mountains can have the layering become vertical as the mass of rock is thrust upward.

figure | 6-27 |

Natural rock formations.

heat and pressure into a new form of rock. Each has its own particular appearance, and should be researched thoroughly. It would be just as erroneous to put a sandstone layered rock formation on a Hawaiian volcano as it would to place a volcano in the middle of Kansas. Some examples of larger and smaller formations are shown below.

No matter what the source, the methodology for drawing these forms is identical to drawing any other subject. In a more subtle way, perspective still must be accounted for in these drawings, and atmospheric perspective, or the loss of color and tonal intensity as the objects are seen further in the distance, should be employed.

The use of natural rock and soil formations to enhance a scene takes on the same dynamic as any other visual element. Does it enhance and belong to the scene and story?

Aerial perspective views over a cliff can give the viewer a delicious vertigo.

Because of their scale and placement, these elements will affect the light and dark of the scene, so be careful of their placement. Ruins can segue into rock formations, giving a surreal feel to a story. The architecture of the Mesoamerican civilizations comes to mind when vegetation and ruins meld.

One final quandary is this: should a larger, close-up element be placed against a broad, partly detailed background? For example, having a menacing sandstone structure placed close to the viewer with a panoramic view of a chasm behind can give a sense of foreground, middle ground, and background in a way that allows dramatic action in the foreground without losing the larger context.

figure | 6-28 |

Aerial perspective with character
in rocky chasm.

The possible kinds of scenes are limitless.

It will be fairly obvious now that the principles given earlier about drawing in general will relate as well to drawing architectural elements, landscapes, and other non-character subjects. All of these provide the context for the action of animation, whether traditional 2D or computer generated or a hybrid of the two.

figure | 6-29 |

Foreground, middle ground, and background
in a scenic drawing.

WATERY

Our topic of animation drawing as it relates to environments would not be complete without
a brief discussion of water. Please note, however, that water is invariably going to be an animated effect and not a simple, static scenic element.

Water effects in drawing are more limited, basically due to the inherent nature of color to
dominate water as a defining characteristic. What you will find iş that there are two basic considerations when drawing water. The first is its structure, and the second is its reflective capa-
bility. Since water takes the form of whatever surface it finds itself on, large bodies of standing water are level unless agitated by wind or objects plunging in and out of or gliding on the

surface. Wind-produced forms can vary greatly, both by the severity of the wind and by the amount of water available. Think of one-hundred-foot waves in the ocean, the so-called freak solitons, versus a pretty good whitecap in the local fishing pond. Water in a spoon or standing in puddles or droplets may have a curved surface, which reflects light in unexpected ways and also transmits it through the water. This causes "hot" spots and uneven lighting, which must be studied in the source itself for authenticity. All water illustration demands research from real sources. Common factors that show up often are curved lines and tonal areas along with sharp changes in light and dark. Reflections follow the general rules of perspective when seen on larger scales, such as a boat dock reflected in a fishing lake. Depending upon the eye level, more or less of the reflected objects will be visible in the water. Any interruption of the surface by other objects or color or debris on the water surface will merely interrupt the image, not change it. Waves and other disturbances will distort the reflected image in the pat-

figure | 6-30

Water as a primary part of the scenic design.

figure | 6-31

Various examples of scenic designs
utilizing multiple elements.

tern of the turbulence; turbulence can make a reflection sometimes appear longer than normal. A water droplet on a tabletop also may transmit a small "spotlight," and this is one of the cues as to its identity. Running water and splashes and drips are special cases that require finding some simple means of repeated animated motion to reproduce; they often show up as cycles in animation because of their complexity, and rarely last a long time for the same reason. There are effects specialists in animation, who know clever ways of mimicking water. CGI (computer-based imagery) has introduced a whole spate of water effects, and has revolutionized the reality of this area of animation. As in all animation-drawing issues, water use should only push the story line along, enhancing the dramatic action or mood of the scene. When it dominates, the domination should be because it is in fact the focal point. See figure 6-30 for samples of water as a drawing subject.

CHAPTER SUMMARY

Key to the skill set of the animation artist is the knowledge and understanding of the general concepts behind creating functional 2D animation backgrounds. The ability for an animation artist to be a keen observer of life and the world around him/her is critical to the rendering of scenic elements. Drawing rock formations, vegetation, water, and other key scenic elements requires a working knowledge of perspective, spatial depth, and how cinematographic concepts affect framing the action of shot-specific backgrounds.

exercises

1. Practice drawing very short (one to two minute) gestures of local houses and buildings, emphasizing basic form over detail. Do the same with natural scenic elements, such as greenery, water, and rock formations.

2. Using photographic reference depicting a variety of architectural subjects (such as Gothic cathedrals, log cabins, and ancient Egyptian temples), try combining different visual elements (like a Tudor house with medieval stone turrets) to create fantastic edifices.

3. Sketch an architectural or natural scenic subject from a variety of distances, with the main subject represented as a foreground, middle ground, and background element in relation to the scenic elements around it.

4. Sketch an architectural or natural scenic subject from different vantage points, such as high angle and low angle views.

5. Sketch an architectural or natural scenic subject at a variety of times during the day (and night) to visualize how various forms of lighting impact scenic elements.

6. Create a series of background drawings with tissue or acetate overlays containing characters, foreground scenic elements, and middle ground scenic elements in order to visualize overall scenic layout.

in review

1. What are the three perspective systems?

2. What are scenic elements and what would be some examples of such elements?

3. What is meant by framing the action in relation to a background?

4. How is character blocking in a scene related to background design?

5. What is the definition of the Rule of Thirds?

THE ANSWER LIES IN THE QUESTION

Richard Wilde

Richard Wilde is the chair of the Graphic Design and Advertising departments at the School of Visual Arts in New York City. Richard is also an accomplished author and a member of HOW Magazine's *Editorial Advisory Board.*

Whenever you embark upon solving a visual communication problem, you fall prey to the usual response of looking for the answer. This response is a habitual knee-jerk reaction, which is the great pitfall of creative thinking and leads to hackneyed solutions that reside in the known. Because if you look for answers, you are mining the area of the brain for what you already know and that in itself negates the creative act.

Curiously enough, if you move in the opposite direction and look for questions instead of answers, your possibilities can take root. It is here where new and innovative solutions arise. Yet resistance to finding the appropriate question lies in the fear of moving into the unknown. We are uncomfortable in this area. Fear of failure looms over us. We are at the mercy of wanting immediate results, which the realm of answers provides.

Finding a meaningful question that ignites interest creates the condition that permits new solutions to arise. In essence, moving into a state of questioning is where creativity can flourish. This, in turn, leads to wonder, a state of openness in which new ideas take form. To wonder is our birthright, and very young children enjoy this capacity. The condition of wonder—not knowing, playing, fooling around and looking with an open mind—is the key to problem solving, for it allows solutions to simply present themselves.

A period of pondering, reflection, introspection and digestion allows the subconscious to make new connections and, hence, original concepts. The greater the priority a question takes, the greater the possibilities. A burning question is fueled by your emotions.

When problem solving, you might suffer from the habit of daydreaming and fantasizing. It takes discipline to simply keep your attention on a given problem, to struggle to be present in the moment using questioning as your anchor. This is a most difficult task.

Don't waste time. Cut to the chase. Probe the problem. Ask questions. Ask more questions. Let questions arise in you. Be diligent. Be merciless. Be serious. Research the problem with a questioning mind. Embrace the process, for it is the struggle of questioning that will feed you, nourish you and make the activity of being a visual communicator truly worthwhile.

In the executional stage, questioning must again be brought in on all decisions concerning color, scale, texture, cropping, composition, tension, rhythm, space, and any other aspects concerning form. For example: the overriding concept might dictate a specific background color. However, what should the intensity be? Should the color be flat? Does it need texture? Should it move from light to dark? Does it work with the rest of the composition? Is the shape of interest? Is the composition too fussy? Is it unresolved? Feel each question. Sense each question. This is where the key lies. It is here where your search unfolds.

To be creative, you must continually struggle against your habitual nature and use the impulse of looking for answers as a warning to move in the opposite direction. The answer can always be found in the question. So ask. And ask. And ask.

what a character!

objectives

introduction

How do you get the idea for a great character? How do you get the idea for any character, for that matter? The fact is that original character ideas can be hard to come by in a world where we are blitzed by a plethora of comic books, animated TV shows, and films, not to mention Internet "webisodes." It is difficult to not be derivative in our character designs, even as we strive for some level of originality in our designs. We may borrow themes and ideas, but should never copy the works of others.

Here are some methods/resources that the authors have found useful for cultivating character concepts.

MYTHOLOGICAL AND EPIC LITERATURE

The folklore and religions of past cultures are swarming with monsters and heroes, ready to be developed into animation characters. Greek mythology has given us Hercules, the Minotaur, Medusa, and the Hydra. Japanese folklore has produced the kappa, the ki-rin, and dragons. Mesopotamian epic literature has given birth to the hero Gilgamesh. Many of these fantastic characters have already been brought to life through the medium of animation, but an exciting and different twist or variation (like a *female* Minotaur) can breathe new life into some old standbys.

figure | 7-1

Female Minotaur.

NOTE

Myths are generally stories from prerational cultures that deal with serious subjects, such as creation, seasonal variations (and the ability to survive them), and so on. Folklore or folktales are, for the most part, less ambitious and often less serious in their scope, often telling stories more localized in nature. The dividing line between the two is arbitrary at best, and many of the most fascinating characters derived from myth can stand alone as subjects for study and entertainment. Epic tales often deal with the hero, and his/her quest for something sacred, as it relates to the survival of their people. Variants of this theme blend with historically ancient events to produce elaborate stories that have features both real and imaginary.

CAFÉ DRAWINGS

Caricature is one of the most powerful tools in the animator's arsenal. Use exaggeration to modify the existing features of actual people to create preliminary character designs. Enlarge noses, lips, and ears; add pigtails, beetling brows, and a nose ring.

Regular trips to the mall or coffee shop could provide a wide variety of people whose local color often needs little exaggeration to create interesting characters. Oftentimes, the features of an individual may suggest an animal form: piggish eyes or an ape-like brow. Human movement is important to observe. Someone may step gingerly like a feline, hobble along stiffly like a robot, or flex their bony arms in a fashion that resembles the motions of a praying mantis.

These visual elements can be the jumping-off point for developing character ideas and become part of the character concept sketch process.

figure | 7-2 |

Exaggeration in character design
based on reality.

figure | 7-3 |

Similarities in design!

THE "WANDERING PENCIL"

This exercise is very effective as a tool for brainstorming on paper, loosening up those drawing muscles, and getting rid of artist's block. It's like a self-generated Rorschach test, only we look at scribbles instead of inkblots.

Place your pencil point on a piece of paper and draw a series of loose scribbles without lifting the lead.

When finished, lift the pencil and observe the gestural form that you've drawn. What do you see? Look for the suggestion of faces or figures in the scribbles. Trace over your rudimentary character scribble with a heavier pencil line or retrace it onto tracing paper.

Use this drawing as a concept sketch from which to further develop your discovered character idea (see figure 7-6).

figure | **7-4** |

Wandering pencil (scribble).

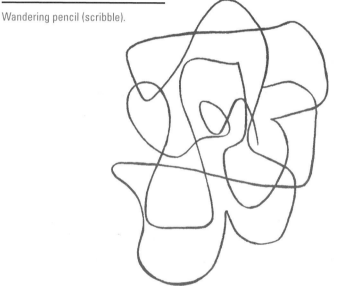

figure | **7-5** |

Modified scribble.

figure | 7-6 |

Character derived from scribble.

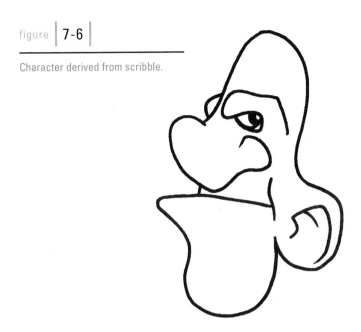

Sometimes it will take dozens and dozens of scribbles before you see anything that you can use. Just keep scribbling!

BRAINSTORMING!

Another fun activity an artist can perform during the creative process of character design is allowing their imagination to run wild and go crazy visually. Getting the ideas out of your head and onto the page is the first step in character creation. This is concept sketching: putting everything you know about a given character down on paper in image form. This is the process of visualization where the animator describes the visual elements that make up the character. Anatomy, costuming, and props are a few of the basic ingredients of the character concept sketch process. The concept sketch can range from a rudimentary thumbnail image to more fully developed character imagery. Here are some examples of concept sketches for character development.

As you begin to visualize your character through drawing, ask questions and try as many variations on a theme as possible. Is the character male or female? Does it wear a hat? Is it bipedal? Does it carry a laser rifle? Does it have the head of a rhinoceros? Do a series of drawings where you vary the elements that make up the character until you get the right mix. Concept sketching is brainstorming with pictures.

figure | 7-7 |

Concept character sketches.

Keep on Sketching!

Here's a trade secret: The three most important tools for the animation artist are 1) pencil, 2) paper, and 3) PRACTICE!!!

Any good artist keeps a sketchbook. Not only does sketching keep our drawing skills honed, but our sketchbooks become reference manuals, filled with visual ideas for use in some future painting, book illustration, animated film, and so on. Sketchbooks can provide visual stimulus for new ideas, as well as keeping a record of old ideas.

Keep a character sketchbook. The character sketchbook is where you should draw any concepts that you have that are character-related: anatomy, costuming, equipment, locations, props, and vehicles. Sidekicks and associated creatures, too! Make drawings and notes on every aspect of character design that pops into your head. Keep this sketchbook near your bed; many times you'll wake up with a great idea, but don't get it down on paper before it's forgotten. Get a small sketchbook so you can keep it with you during your waking hours.

Draw! Draw! Draw! Good drawing habits stimulate skill and the imagination.

LOOKIN' GOOD...OR BAD!

Characters drive story. If we want the audience to care about our story, we require characters that are suitable for delivering that message. Exciting and well-planned character design is the key. Let us consider a very important character design element. Before putting pencil to paper, the following attributes should be taken into account in any character creation process.

Visual Appeal/Dynamics:

The indispensable book *The Illusion of Life* describes *appeal* as "anything that a person likes to see, a quality of charm, pleasing design, simplicity, communication, and magnetism. Your eye is drawn to the figure that has appeal, and, once there, it is held while you appreciate what you are seeing." Characters represent ideals, and so a general rule we can apply to their design is that a hero should be heroic, a villain villainous, a fairy tale princess beautiful, and a monster ugly. *Character design should reflect a character's physical and moral attributes.* Now having said that, let us consider the fact that some evil characters are pretty or charming and some incredibly powerful characters are scrawny or dinky (Hanna Barbera's Atom Ant). Certain story lines may dictate this kind of scenario. Disney's Quasimodo proves that ugliness does not always equal meanness. We can bend the rules of character design once we understand how to apply them. The intrigue or comedy stylings in a plot line will often create parameters for twists in character design. Characters whose appearance or morality changes outside of the story line lack credibility.

Next to a boring story, a boring character (or characters) can spell the demise of an animated film. We want the audience to be interested in the characters we display and to empathize with them. Animation is a visual medium, so the characters should be visually interesting. Characters are attention-grabbers. The audience wants stimulating and credible characters. If the viewer perceives some problem with a character, such as design, anatomy, or movement issues, he/she will unfortunately have difficulty suspending disbelief and will lose interest in the story. Therefore, we see that character design can have a direct effect on the functionality of the story.

Appropriate Style

The visual style of the character should fit the visual style of the production. For example, Hanna Barbera's Fred Flintstone would look very odd juxtaposed against the characters and backgrounds from Ralph Bakshi's animated adaptation of Tolkien's *Lord of the Rings*. A corollary of appropriate style is the simplification of character line and detail in preparation for animation: minimized character detail equals streamlined animation drawing.

THE ANIMATOR
AT WORK

Hayao Miyazaki

Among the most renown of Japan's animators is Hayao Miyazaki. Born in Tokyo in 1941, he is currently one of the premier artists in Japan's animation industry. He became interested in animation when, as a third-year high school student, he saw the anime film *Hakuja Den* (the first feature-length anime film). Fascinated by the stylized faces and lush backgrounds common to the genre, Hayao began his career as a cartoonist and future animator.

At Gakushuin University, while studying economics, he joined the Children's Literature

Research Club, which was as close to cartooning and related artistic ventures as the school offered. Although graduating with degrees in Economics and Political Science, Miyazaki went immediately to Toei Animation, in 1963. At this time, he was still an in-betweener, working on such features as *Watchdog Bow Wow,* and the television series *Wolf Boy Ken.*

By 1965, Miyazaki was an animator on *Prince of the Sun,* (1968) and later that year was a key animator on *Puss in Boots.* With his wife Akemi, Hayao contributed significantly to the film *The Flying Ghost Ship.*

In 1971, Miyazaki joined A-Pro studio. During this time he worked heavily in television animation series. This venture lasted only two years, and then while on his own again, he did work for various films as scene designer. Television again lured him, and he was the director for *Conan, The Boy in Future.* Finally, the chance to direct a film by himself occurred when Tokyo Movie Shinsha hired him to direct his first movie, *Lupin III: The Castle of Cagliostro.* Manga comics also consumed much of his time, and eventually he released *Nausicaa of the Valley of Wind,* an animation film based upon a Manga comic. Now at the newly established Studio Ghibli, Miyazaki began writing, directing, and producing such films as the immensely successful *Princess Mononoke,* released in the states by Disney. His latest effort, the beautiful and mysterious *Spirited Away,* broke the record for highest grossing film in Japanese history, formerly held by his own *Princess Mononoke.* He is best known for his extremely entertaining and involved plots, along with superb animation and unusual and interesting characters.

Alignment

Back to those moral attributes, a character's goodness or evil intentions should be recognized as a part of design and thus be incorporated. You must make a decision as to whether or not these morals manifest themselves physically or as part of the character's mental make-up or both. This will help determine how the character will be drawn.

Casting

If the production calls for a hero, don't create a villain for the part. A mighty barbarian who swings a seventy-pound battle-axe should appear appropriately burly. Create a character capable of fulfilling his/her or its role in the film. This sounds like common sense, but should always be a checkpoint in character creation.

The Twist

Effective characters often incorporate unexpected elements in their make-up, either physically, mentally, emotionally, or as a combination of any of these elements. A character that appears to be human may be disguising a plethora of slimy tentacles and a pair of distinctly dinosaurian hind legs under his long, black trench coat. A character that seems sweet and timid could be hiding a diabolically evil personality.

The Silhouette

Someone once said that *a great character has a unique silhouette.* That means we could recognize them by their shadow cast on a wall.

figure | 7-8 |

Character defined by silhouette.

Immediate character recognition is valuable as it not only differentiates characters in the same story from each other (all of them shouldn't look alike anyway), but it also separates them from their "competitors," in the animation genre. *Silhouetting in animation also refers to designing poses in an animation sequence that allow the character action to be "read" by the audience.* For instance, if our character is a space ranger preparing to draw his laser pistol from its holster, the audience needs to be able to clearly see the character's movement to understand the action. This means the animator must display an unobscured view of the weapon, the character's move to unholster it, and the readiness of the space ranger's stance. If we silhouette the aforementioned pose, we should be able to clearly see the action without the need for detail.

EARLY TYPECASTING

Here are some examples of character types whose designs are based strictly on related physiology and/or a generalization of character.

The Hybrid

The satyr from ancient Greek mythology would be a good example of this design form.

A hybrid character is a mix of different physiological attributes from two or more different types of life forms (or mechanisms, in the case of a cyborg character). In other words, a mix and match of body parts from different types of creatures. We often see such character designs that mix animals and humans (satyr = goat parts + human parts), animals with other animals . . . and organic beings with mechanical elements.

figure | **7-9** |

Hybrid design form.

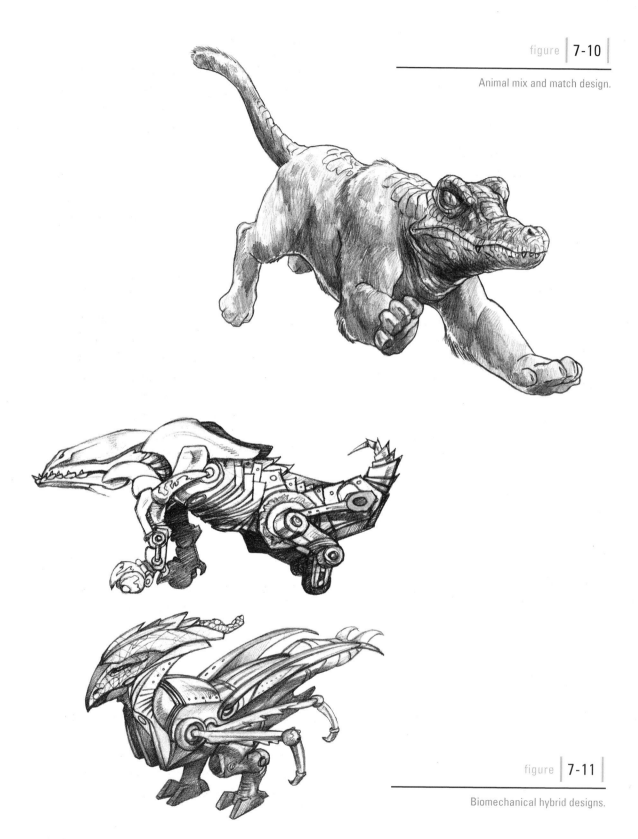

figure | 7-10 |

Animal mix and match design.

figure | 7-11 |

Biomechanical hybrid designs.

figure | 7-12 |

Archetypal hero.

The Archetype

Villain, hero, monster, clown, or damsel in distress—the archetype characters are cross-cultural stereotypes found in traditional legends and tales. A "knight in shining armor" of Arthurian legend would qualify as an archetype hero.

In the case of these characters, the concept of stereotype refers to a standardization of attributes and appearance applied to the aforementioned character forms.

The Usually Inanimate Character

Another type of character is an inanimate object brought to life, typically imbued with some human-like characteristics that allow us to emotionally connect with this sort of character form. It could be a happy harp or a surly stone, perhaps. How about an automobile, a tree, or an apple?

Disney's flying carpet character in the animated film *Aladdin* would be a good example of this character type.

The Animal

How about an animal character with anthropomorphic (human-like) attributes: speech, an upright posture, human intellect, humanoid physique, and so on.

This is a character type that is commonly portrayed in animated films. Although it goes without saying, the trick to doing a good animal character is to be as original as possible. As animator Don Bluth once mentioned at a seminar, "A mouse is among the most difficult of animals to bring to life as character because so many animated mice have already been done."

figure | 7-13

Inanimate objects as characters.

ANATOMICALLY SPEAKING...

In Chapter 3, we talked about anatomy in a fairly objective way; that is, discussing what an ulna is, where it is located, and what it does. Without this knowledge, it would be difficult to understand or construct authentic-looking drawings that lead to character development. Artists learning the craft can be roughly divided into two groups. The first group works entirely on instinct and avoids much study on such things as anatomy, perspective, and the like. The second group is more thorough, involving themselves in life drawing and similar disciplines. There is no guarantee that a brilliant talent will not evolve from the first group, or a dull and uninspired artist from the second, but history has shown in the workplace that the best artists almost always come from the second batch, and the reason is simple: with more knowledge, more is possible. Anatomy is a core element in this success. Why? Because *all character form is first derived from some possible anatomical model.* Even cartoon characters still obey certain

figure | 7-14 |

Anthropomorphic character.

rules derived from the study of muscle and bone. More specific knowledge is necessary for realistic character development, as when the artist might wish to construct a Viking, road-runner, or octopoid. False steps in drawing body shapes could yield humorous and even hysterical consequences.

When drawing cartoon characters, artists need to pay more attention to basic shapes based upon anatomy. The number of ribs is not as important as the basic rib cage shape; the exact relationship of tibia to fibula is subordinate to the asymmetric inside and outside curves of the lower leg. In very reductive cartoons, where the forms have become extremely generic, it is often the proportional relationships between head and body or legs and torso that become essential to the drawing.

Movement is the other issue touched by anatomy. As a famous Disney animator once stated, "All movement starts at the hips." Having at least a cursory understanding of this area, including its relationship to the rest of the body, and the general articulation of each area of the body will give much greater "realness" to character movement. Even cartoon animation acknowledges general anatomical limitations, albeit with a great deal of leeway. We talked about movement in several previous chapters, and Chapter 3 dealt in greater detail with anatomy and its effect on movement. *In character development, the animation artist doesn't just have to account for a static image of the character, but must also think in terms of how it will move, as well.* It is possible to design an extremely interesting-looking alien character that can't move at all. It all has to do with internal design, an issue usually overlooked by beginners (and sometimes ignored by professionals). Internal design merely means thinking in terms of the anatomical element. Such a design works best when based upon real anatomy, because we can predict action by watching and analyzing people and nature. Fantastic creatures and similar ilk are often either amazing products or unfortunate victims of this internal design issue. We are reminded again of dragons that can't fly, and of creatures that have no digestive tracts or other needed parts. This does not mean that such characters are forbidden. Quite the contrary! But we need to convince the audience that the character moves and operates in a way that seems authentic. Again, character design should reflect credible anatomical structure, even when exaggerated. This adds an air of believability to the design. This form of observation is especially critical when an artist begins to design characters that are based on other living forms, such as animals and plants or hybrids of both. When you look at the drawings of people like Disney animator Glenn Keane and fantasy illustrators Frank Frazetta and Heinrich Kley, it is obvious that these individuals have observed and learned the structure of human and animal anatomy and can apply it. One must imagine that even cartoon characters have an underlying anatomy of bones, muscles, and organs, so that these basic anatomical principles of anatomy and movement can be applied, even if in an exaggerated manner. Drawing and studying humans and animals from life (along with imagination) is the key to effective character design.

The point is that the audience will recognize a lack of knowledge and/or skill on the part of the animator if they notice problems in applied character anatomy or movement. Master stop-motion animator Ray Harryhausen once remarked that he preferred animating imaginary creatures to animating versions of living animals (like the elephant in his film *Twenty Million Miles to Earth*). He mentioned that people are familiar with how animal movement looks (whether they understand it entirely or not), and that they will more readily see the flaws in the animation of such characters than in the animation of mythical ones—no one has ever seen the movements of a dragon or a monster from Venus.

Drawing and studying human and animal anatomy/motion from life is the key to effective character design and to making the characters appear plausible to the audience. These are the issues that inexorably link life drawing to character design and animation.

FAMOUS LAST WORDS

Let's summarize our foray into character creation.

Do's and Don'ts of Character Design

Do:

- Simplify anatomy and visual detail.
- Design the character according to the part he/she/it plays in the story. Create credible physical and moral attributes.
- Use a variety of visual and literary sources for character reference and inspiration.
- Participate in a lot of written and drawn brainstorming about characters.
- Practice your drawing skills.

Don't:

- Create visually uninteresting characters.
- Compromise the visual style of your story with a character design that doesn't fit: realistic vs. cartoony.
- Give the character an unmanageable amount of appendages/extremities, clothing, or equipment.
- Copy the character designs of other artists. Respect copyrights!

CHAPTER SUMMARY

Research and brainstorming on paper are key elements in character concept creation. Regular sketching, along with exercises such as the "wandering pencil," help to develop and hone the character design skills of the animation artist. The rules of style and visual appeal, along with a working knowledge of anatomy, are critical factors in creating animation characters that help to drive the story and hold audience interest.

exercises

1. Do several café drawings and try modifying the anatomical features of each figure to create a series of character concept sketches.

2. Do several animal studies in both quick sketch format and a more finished form. Choosing the best among these, transform two of these into animal variations of the original animal; then change one of the animals more radically so that it will be a derivative of the original animal.

3. From exercise 2, take two animals and combine features from each to produce a new animal; then take this animal and modify it further using single feature changes at a time.

4. Combine one of the animal sketches and human forms into a hybrid animal/human character.

5. Retrace a series of concept drawings of a character. Ink these drawings solidly black to observe how silhouetting works as a design element for these character studies.

in review

1. Describe the wandering pencil exercise.

2. How would you define a concept sketch?

3. What is meant by the term visual appeal?

4. What role does the silhouette play in character design?

character construction 101

objectives

introduction

Once we've ironed out the basic idea for our character design through concept sketches, the next step is to refine the sketch into a more fully rendered, comprehensive version of what the final character will look like. This refinement will ultimately lead to the development of the model sheet.

The idea of the refined character sketch is to lock-in a final design by correcting and finalizing anatomical detail and proportion, attitude/expressions, costuming, accessories, and so on. Refinement in character drawing is also a clean-up process, whereby we eliminate extraneous construction lines and "dirty" marks from the drawing, while emphasizing and strengthening line work that is crucial to defining volume and anatomy. Retracing your concept sketch on another sheet of paper is a good way to refine the form and make lines crisp. Here's an example of a concept sketch and a refined version of the same character.

Even though we're going to simplify the character later, we keep full detail at the refined sketch level.

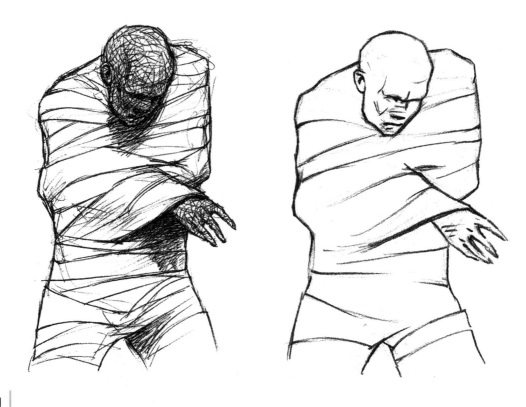

figure | 8-1 |

Rough illustration cleaned up for animation.

STEREOTYPING

As we know, real-life reference is of paramount importance to character design, but it's also important to define the character elements that restrict a character design. Once you've established these elements, the real-life observation of the figure will help you to modify them into a good character design. Meanwhile, here are some examples and suggestions based on generalized character types.

The Brute

Often used as the "heavy" or comedic oaf, strength and low intelligence are the primary attributes of the brutish character. Essentially, we're putting together visual elements that create the stereotype of physical power and dumbness.

- A small head equals a small brain.
- Big chest, big shoulders, and big arms. The brute may be muscular like a body-builder or show strength with proportional mass (i.e., gorilla-sized arms on a normal, human-sized character).
- Large hands make it easier to grab big, heavy objects.
- Bandy legs and large feet. The greater the bend at the knees, the heavier the character appears. Big feet support the weight.
- Small, close-set eyes suggest a low intellect.
- The more the character's back is hunched, the more apish and less man-like he/she/it appears.

figure | 8-2 |

The Brute.

The Clown/Fool/Trickster

These characters are comedic foils, pranksters, sympathetic oafs, and sometimes sidekicks. The clown appears as a character in virtually every culture on the planet. Coyote, Loki, Mr. Punch, Simple Simon, and the medieval court jester are examples of all the parts of this character form. These figures often provide a humorous or clever diversion within the principal drama of the story. The clown may also be an antagonist. The clown character is most effectively divided into the "fool" and "trickster" stereotypes. The following physical elements define these characters.

The Fool

- Sloping forehead and small head equal low intellect.
- Clownish nose
- Chinless
- Buckteeth
- Large hands and feet
- Gangly limbs
- Slouching posture

figure | 8-3 |

Clown/fool.

The Trickster

It is difficult to pin down the characteristics of the Trickster as they come in a wide variety of cultural manifestations. The following information sums up some of the commonalities that can be attributed to the tricksters found in world mythologies.

- He/she/it may be a shape-shifter, capable of taking on a variety of forms, such as those of a human, animal or natural phenomena.

- This character often takes the form of animals that display humorous antics or appear to act or move strangely (monkeys and bats) and/or are known for their cunning in hunting prey/escaping predators (foxes and rabbits).

- He/she/it may have magical powers and appear as a jester/bard type of character.

- Makes sly and furtive movements.

- Plays pranks.

The Heroic Male and Female

Heroic animation characters represent larger-than-life archetype protagonists. Strength, intelligence and, typically, ideal physical form are the mainstays of the hero's attributes. The hero must appear to be able to vanquish the villain through force or virtue, although some "anti-heroes" may not fit the aforementioned heroic mold. The hero plays against the antagonist to restore order, and thus *piloting* the dramatic vehicle that drives the story. The heroic animation character can typically be defined by the following characteristics.

figure | 8-4

The Trickster.

Traditional Heroic Male

- Idealized anatomy: overall proportions are more substantial than on the average human male. Wide shoulders and a narrow waist suggest fitness and a strong frame.

- Muscular body

- The heroic character may be very tall and displays a straight, imposing posture.

- Square jaw

- Well-groomed

- Strong, attractive/ pleasant features

figure | 8-5 |

Heroic male character.

Traditional Heroic Female

- 'Amazon-like' proportions
- Muscular or well-toned body. May have an "hourglass" figure.
- May have relatively small hands and feet.
- Wide shoulders
- Well-groomed/attractive

As with any archetypes based on myth, legend, or popular culture, the hero is a stereotypical model that may be modified by specific cultural beliefs and lifestyles.

figure | 8-6 |

Heroic female character.

SIMPLIFY!

The production of a 2D animated feature film requires a tremendous amount of drawing, from concept sketches and layout to the final clean-up drawings. This means that thousands of drawings of character animation are required. It would be incredibly difficult to animate a character like this one.

figure | 8-7 |

Difficult character to animate.

Complex characters sporting a great deal of detail are not going to be suitable candidates for animation. Why? Lack of simplification is the reason. It is too technically difficult and expensive to deal with all of the details in a feature film. We will discuss this more later in the book.

Character realism and character simplification are, in some ways, the most important issues facing a designer. This is because it has to do with what you are trying to say with a particular character. Does it fit into the story? Do all the characters look like they belong in the same story? Is the character effective in the way it was designed, or can it be improved. There are endless modifications of characters in studios as they develop their products. And finally, does it function within an animation context? What is partly meant by this is the concept of *thresholds*. Humans (and actually all creatures) operate within their environments by means of thresholds, that is, levels of information. We actually only need a modest amount of information to function: two dots and a curved line for a mouth have become symbolic for a face (as seen in the ubiquitous, yellow "smiley face" design), and we react to it as such. That kind of reaction is hard-wired in the brain.

Adding too much information drowns the viewer with unnecessary things to process, and the character is lost. If too little information is presented, the character will not be fully understood. This is further complicated by whether you intend a realistic character or simpler (perhaps cartoon) character. In each case, different levels of information are needed. A cartoon character seems ludicrous when developed in the same way as a totally real CGI character. And there is the functional problem: too much information is impossible to animate. You simply can't draw all of those details, frame after frame, and even in computer animation, economics prohibits too much detail. It is simply too expensive and time consuming to render more than a certain level of information. This, coupled with the fact that our brains do just fine with a little bit of visual information, gives us a kind of rough formula for constructing characters. Realistic characters need more information, but *not* insane amounts; cartoon and stylized characters need less information (detail), but *enough* to make the viewer believe. Sketchbooks are full of attempts at all different levels of detail, and they *should* be. There should be scores of alternate investigations into different character designs. When this is done, the artists themselves can judge whether they have gone too far, missed the mark altogether, or have a winner. They should then show their designs to teachers, other artists, and peers in general to get a consensus as to their success.

Let's define simplification for animation before we go any further. It is the process by which animation artists refine a character design by strengthening line quality and reducing unnecessary figurative detail. The *purpose of simplification is to help assure continuity;* it's easier and more straightforward for the animators to draw a character with less detail, and it conserves drawing time for the same reason. We can reduce detail and line work (from a *refined* character concept drawing) in the following areas:

· muscular detail

· hair detail

· wrinkles and folds in clothing

· skin or surface texture

figure | 8-8 |

Simplification of character for animation purposes.

Here we can see the process of creating a character design that is suitable for animation by refinement and simplification.

Characters are symbols; the audience needs a good set of visual clues to recognize and accept the character as a certain type: heroic knight, cute baby, or fierce dragon. We need not render every scale on the dragon's back or costume the cavalier in 14th-century German parade armor in order to develop him/her as an acceptable character.

A QUICK MENTION OF COLOR

Color palettes are also simplified for animation characters. For each color, we will have only three tones to represent it (base color, highlight, and shadow). If this were not the case, animation characters would have to be painted in continuous tones, with colors blending seamlessly into one another. Traditionally, this concept has been too much work and too costly. More importantly, it would be difficult to maintain color continuity with continuous color. As the world of digital coloring in animation advances, we will certainly be seeing the use of extended, complex color palettes.

EXAGGERATION, OR "SWALLOW THAT KERNEL OF TRUTH"

Throughout this tome, we've addressed the need for the animator to observe and learn the structure of human and animal anatomy. This knowledge and the ability to be a good observer provide the artist with a firm, realistic foundation upon which to build his/her drawing skills. Having said that, we'll contradict ourselves again and tell you that the *exaggeration* of anatomy and movement are of great importance to the art of (cartoon) animation.

Actually, once we have a good understanding of the anatomical structure of living beings and their locomotion, we can take that information and stretch the limits of realism and drama in animation. *Know* the rules, *then* break them!

What exactly do we mean by exaggeration? We mean the process by which the animator overemphasizes movement and form to clearly convey specific actions, emotions, and characterization to the audience. As observers of animation, we have a tendency to change gears, mentally, and look at form and movement differently from when we look at real life or when we view live-action cinema. We accept subtlety of acting, form, and movement in real life and the cinema, but require extreme versions of these elements in animation in order to have them come across correctly on screen. Acting in animation relies a great deal on the necessary melodrama that continues to be an acting staple in many aspects of modern theatre. In order for the entire audience to be able to comprehend the play, the actor must be able to convey emotion, even to the person seated in the farthest balcony. This same concept applies to the nature of exaggeration in animation.

With exaggeration of form, *extreme extremities* is the rule of the day! Fat, skinny, tall, short, ugly, muscular—all elements of anatomy peculiar to both humans and animals. Even some extreme conditions in these areas of physiology don't come close to the kind of caricature that we can create by pushing the form farther and farther visually. The realistically overweight person in the first figure does not convey extreme obesity, as does the exaggerated character in the second figure.

figure | 8-9 |

Realistic sketch of an overweight person.

figure | 8-10 |

Cartoon version of an overweight person.

Visual extremes in the design of animated characters will make a greater impression on the audience than a moderate style. Don't say fat, say **FAT!!!** If obesity is an important characterization element, push the fatness to the max!

The same concept holds true for muscularity. Compare the following realistic figure to the extremely muscular character.

Once again, we've pushed the anatomical envelope to provide interesting characterization.

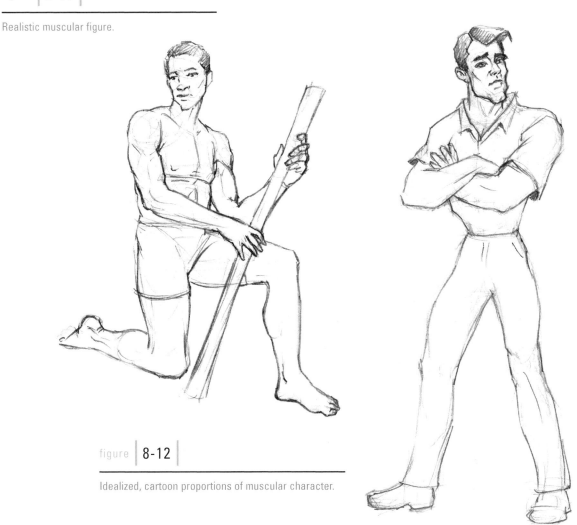

figure | 8-11 |

Realistic muscular figure.

figure | 8-12 |

Idealized, cartoon proportions of muscular character.

WHAT'S MY (CONTOUR) LINE?

Contour is a convention that allows us to describe form and volume through an exterior line and is of great importance in simplification and editing information about characters and other animation elements. Contour line has certain defined tasks. One is to contain the form, that is, where its apparent boundaries are in relation to the background. Another is to indicate structural change, such as a line for the edge of a cube separating two planes. Lines also are used for pattern and texture, but as such are not really as important as contour lines. With this in mind, simplification, as related to animation, allows the artist more freedom in animation because less information has to be manipulated in each drawing. More detail equals more time drawing. Cartoons also require a kind of economy of line as well, because we are dwelling only on the exaggerated bits of information. Their style becomes paramount. The whole thing boils down to, in a funny way, the "kinks" in the line.

Lines have direction, curvature, focus, thickness or thinness, and fragmentary or multiple elements. With these qualities manipulated in combination, many varied types of messages are possible. A very powerful short animation about Sisyphus (the mythological character doomed to getting an enormous boulder to the top of a mountain over and over again for eternity) that was done some years ago, combined bold, heavy, stylized line and an expressive sound track to portray the mythical character pushing a boulder up a mountain. Every brush stroke of the body enhanced the sense of struggle, weight, and effort by Sisyphus. Had the animation been done with elegant, elongated line, the whole sense of the power of the story would have been lost. Funny or clownish stories often benefit from a fragmentary sort of line, giving minimal information but that which is given being humorous because of its brevity.

figure | 8-13 |

Fragmentary line quality used in cartoon style.

Ultimately, the most useable, multipurpose line is in the variety called thick/thin. The reason for this is obvious: the simple device of changing the weight or thickness of the line can emphasize any change in form. By having line with variation, the form escapes being boring. Overlap and mass can also be hinted at or reinforced by thicker and thinner lines. Cartoons are more interesting when their simplicity is slightly tweaked by change in line quality. This allows for a simple form that still has various looks.

Sometimes, as in life drawing, volume and space are given more substantiality by thick and thin line. Since animation, at its most complex, still involves enormous numbers of images, the solutions to line must remain attainable by both hand and machine. So compromise is in order. Add enough to keep the drawing alive, but don't smother it in nuances. Pencils and charcoal get a flattened edge as they are being used, and this can be used to advantage in making varied lines by merely rotating to the flatter or thinner portion of the point or lead.

No matter what line you choose, it must ultimately be suitable to the subject. Funky, fragmentary lines don't do superheroes justice, and highly simplistic, reductive lines are equally uncomplimentary to realistic rendering. *Good design will be hurt by bad line, but bad design is not rescued by good line.* In the quality of the line work, we must always maintain continuity. As in all things, a complete technique is necessary for success.

LADIES AND GENTLEMEN: THE MODEL SHEET

The culmination of character design for animation comes in the form of the model sheet. *Model sheets are character blueprints.* They describe in exact detail a character's physical appearance based on a variety of proportional views, and often include a selection of images showing the character in different poses or attitudes and various facial expressions. The abil-

figure | **8-14** |

Modified line quality in character.

ity to maintain line width and quality is an important drawing skill necessary for creating model sheets, as their images represent the cleaned-up character designs. Typically, uniform contour line for animation character drawing helps maintain visual continuity, with possible modifications based on specific character design issues. The model sheet is the final, official, "agreed-upon" design for a given character. It is a drawing guide for animators and clean-up artists that ensures design continuity in the character animation.

Model sheets are used to address various character elements like movement and facial features, but the most common and useful variety is known as the "turn-around." The *turn-around* is a model sheet showing three to five proportional, neutral views of the character. The views used in a turn-around are commonly front, 3/4 front (facing the viewer at a 45-degree angle), profile, 3/4 rear (facing away from the viewer at a 45-degree angle), and rear. Each pose is drawn with the character views standing on the same ground plane, helping to maintain height continuity and overall proportion. Model sheets are also available for props for the same purpose, that is, complete understanding in full 360-degree rotation so that all assistant and in-between artists can properly construct each element in the film. Standard and unusual views of backgrounds, although not per se model sheets, serve the same function.

These days, the character is frequently modeled in clay or a hardening sculpting clay as a maquette, or small sculpture, first and then used as the source for drawings. This allows the artists to see the character and all of its particular idiosyncrasies in actual three-dimensional reality. These maquettes are even scanned for use in computer-driven animation. Interestingly, most artists find that sculpting helps their drawing skills, and visa versa.

The height of a character depicted on a turn-around may be measured in heads. A series of parallel lines perpendicular to the character views are drawn behind (or next to) the poses. The space between each line is equal to the measured height of the character's head (crown to chin). This is a useful tool for proportional measurement when drawing a character. An artist may also use a series of parallel lines (erased on the final model sheet) as a drawing guide, measuring the critical placement and height of such anatomical reference points as the top of the head, eyes, chin, bottom of the pectorals, shoulder line, hip line, fingertips, and knee line.

You may run across the term *points* in reference to the turn-around (i.e., a three-point turn-around). The number of points refers to the number of views on the turn-around sheet. A four-point turn-around would mean that four views of that character are shown; these would typically be the front, 3/4 front, profile, and rear views.

figure | **8-15** |

Character model sheet.

Turn-arounds may also contain side drawings, diagrams, and/or text information that give specific instructions on drawing that particular character. There are two other commonly used model sheet forms: action poses and facial expressions. These model sheets help to define characterization by showing a character's style of movements. How does he/she run, hop, or fly? What kind of expressions does he/she make when furious, overjoyed, or disgusted? These questions can be answered visually with such model sheets.

CHAPTER SUMMARY

Exaggeration, character simplification, and model sheet creation are necessary components in the animation character design process. The stereotype as a reference method for creating characters and the exaggeration of anatomical features are also key components in character design. Solid, observational drawing skill and contour line use for refining drawings are important factors in creating simplified characters for use in 2D animation. The understanding of model sheet creation in animation production is a very important technical skill for the animation artist.

exercises

1. Develop a series of character concept sketches based on a character stereo-type, such as oaf, hero, damsel in distress, etc.

2. Based on the drawings generated in exercise 1, create a turn-around for that character.

3. Using the turn-around generated in exercise 2 as reference, create a model sheet that displays this character in a variety of action poses.

4. Retrace some life drawings on another sheet of paper and try exaggerating various anatomical elements (such as the arms, legs, and head), along with perspective and foreshortening modifications. Look for body parts that lend themselves to caricature.

5. Retrace a detailed character drawing of a life drawing on another sheet of paper, and try reducing the line work and detail to create simplified figures. Vary the line quality in these drawings.

in review

1. What is the definition of a turn-around?

2. What is the reason for eliminating excess detail when preparing a character design for animation?

3. What do we mean when we say characters are symbols?

4. How can we use thick/thin line in character design and dramatic action?

5. What are some examples of basic (archetypal) character types?

6. How does exaggeration aid in character construction? Why do we use this technique?

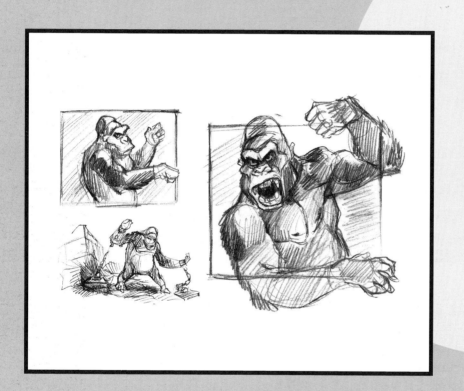

roughing it and cleaning it up!

objectives

Develop an understanding of the nature of rough animation and how to relate quick sketching skills to rough animation

Cultivate a basic understanding of the 2D animation process

Understand the definition of keyframes, clean-up, and in-betweening

Review the concept of dynamic action

Learn the relationship between rough animation and the action path

Learn some introductory hand techniques in 2D animation

Acquire an introduction to the steps used in constructing rough animation

Gain a basic understanding of animation clean-up and the tools used to do it

Discover the relationship of model sheets to clean-up

introduction

One of the biggest problems that budding animators have in producing successful 2D animation is their initial hesitation to starting the process with rough animation, which is the initial gestural animation (for our purposes, character animation) produced for a specific animation sequence. *The reason we do rough animation is to generate the basic character movements and then check to make sure the animation functions correctly.* We seem to be more interested in describing drawn forms using tight detail and contour than with volume and basic structure. Although the look of rough animation will vary from scribbly figures to recognizable character drawings, the concern for detail causes new animators to try creating animation as a series of refined character illustrations. Although the clean-up process is relative to this "illustrative" way of thinking, movement is the important aspect in animation: the creation of figures with believable volume and perspective moving and acting in space. It doesn't matter how good the characters look if their movement is dysfunctional. This is where rough animation comes into play.

ROUGHING IT AND CLEANING IT UP!

LAYING IT ON THE LINE

As in all animation techniques, we start with the story. How we want to tell the story is key. Visuals all spin from this simple premise. After editing and refining the story and turning it into a script, the director is then able to have a storyboard produced, which, as we have seen, is the beginning of real visualization. In the storyboard are proto-characters and backgrounds (along with props) and their first realized relationships. The nature of the specific story and its emotional content guide the artists in their interpretations of the contents. Camera shots define much of what happens, since dialogue should be at a minimum, letting the action propel the story line. Different views of the same background along with the characters can give radically differing emotive contents; for example, a chase scene from a worm's-eye view at an extreme closeup on the feet of the protagonist gives a totally different feel from a long shot where the character is a minor detail of a larger setting. In the first, we are both given and denied information, and that produces anxiety, excitement, curiosity, and the like, whereas in the second version, almost all relevant visual information was provided, leaving the drama strictly to the overall feel of the runner and the background. Of course, both shots can be used together skillfully, to give a sequential exposition of the story. What is important to us as artists, however, is that drawing the character and the backgrounds are far from simple tasks.

Camera shots can define what and how we see a story; movement within a camera shot, or a "traveling" camera shot, using pans, zooms, and similar techniques, also influences what kinds of choices to make regarding the character(s) and background(s). Since we normally perceive our world at standard eye level, any change from this (such as a bird's-eye view) gives a jolt to the contents of a scene, for the simple reason that an element of unfamiliarity has been introduced for all scenic content. Lighting can also have this effect. It has been found that the human brain is apparently hard-wired for light sources to come from above, mimicking sunlight and the sun's position. By placing the light sources at odd angles, especially from below, the brain struggles to match this new light/dark pattern to the familiar forms it normally encounters. In horror, mystery, and suspense stories, this can provide an extraordinarily simple means to produce the mood desired by the artist and director.

Keyframes, sometimes known as key drawings, in 2D animation are important sequential drawings that define major changes in character/object action, creating visual anchor points between which we can establish the rest of the drawings in that chunk of animation. Keyframes establish the timing, character, quality, and dynamics of the animated movement. Key drawings plan out the action. Think of keyframes as the cool and exciting poses that you are developing your drawings toward as you progress through an animated sequence. Sometimes these poses are not particularly action-packed (like a hobo picking up a discarded cigar), but they can and should be chockfull of characterization.

With all of that being said, we are reminded that layout work for backgrounds is an integral element in planning and executing (rough) animation. *Background design directly affects character movement, so a final design for the environment is critical. The character must function in relationship to the background and have planned interaction.* Plotting the animation drawings directly over a background drawing on a lightbox can solve animation and background layout problems.

The following steps present an effective way to envision the process of working through the creation of a 2D animated sequence. This process is derived from Disney's animation procedure, "Seven Steps in Animating a Scene," discussed in the book *The Illusion of Life: Disney Animation.*

1. PLAN: Planning is thinking on paper. Write down a description of the animated scene including basic character, background, and action information.

2. SKETCH: Sketching is further thinking on paper. Draw a series of thumbnail images that define the layout of scenic elements and character interaction for key shots within the sequence.

3. KEY: Create keyframe drawings for the animated sequence by enlarging your thumbnail imagery (via the use of a photocopier or another method) and utilizing those sketches as direct reference for character movement and blocking. Modify these keyframes as necessary, keeping in mind the timing of the action(s).

4. SHOOT: Film, videotape, or digitally capture the keyframes and process them through a pencil-test system (which we will discuss later) so that the images can be viewed sequentially as animation. It is important to carefully observe the timing, action, and drawing quality for any problems.

5. REFINE: Fix any problems in the above-mentioned areas of the key drawing animation.

6. REPEAT: Go back to step 1 and repeat the process until the keyframe animation is working. If the animation functions correctly, you can move on to creating breakdown drawings and in-betweens.

| NOTE |

An In-between Note…

There are two other important types of drawings that fill in the space between those wonderful keyframes in an animated sequence: breakdowns and in-betweens. Breakdown (or "passing position") drawings are placed directly in the middle between two key drawings, showing an intermediate position that the character needs to pass through on his way from one important action to another. And in-betweens are filler drawings created between keyframes and breakdowns that describe the rest of the animated movement.

GESTURING

The process of creating effective 2D animation typically starts with preliminary sketches and thumbnails that describe general character position and action in relationship to the environment.

This concept of rough preliminary sketching is the same idea that we've presented in doing initial drawings of both organic and inorganic forms, like the human figure and architecture.

Preliminary sketch design ideas.

Preliminary design sketch.

Rough thumbnails become references from which you can derive a series of keyframes. You can use a photocopier to enlarge the drawings to an appropriate size to be used for visual reference or as a direct source from which initial key drawings are traced.

Sometimes you might find that you can't remember how a torso looks when it's rotated in a certain direction, how a foot should be foreshortened when viewed from a particular angle, or what a sneer really looks like. To solve these and other problems, the animation artist can and should be working in the life drawing studio, drawing gestures and sequences from a model as direct preparatory reference for animation. Keeping a small mirror in your studio can help you to act out movements and facial expressions.

DYNAMATION!

(Our apologies to stop-motion animation maestro, Ray Harryhausen. "Dynamation" was a name coined by Harryhausen and producer Charles H. Schneer to describe Ray's special effects process by which he composited live action humans into scenes with stop-motion creatures and vice versa.)

We have already talked about the role of dynamic figure and character drawing in Chapter 5 of this book, but we're going to discuss it again because of its important role in rough animation.

Dynamic movement involves many things. It partly refers to what we have already established, that is, line of action and its relation to the static horizontal/vertical context of the monitor or movie screen (screen direction). If action moves parallel to these visual limits, then it can seem (but is not necessarily) restrained. Dynamic movement therefore is partly the direction of movement, which can also be reflected in the actual dominating line of the character itself. It can also refer to the nature of the smaller information we include as we draw a character. What we mean by this is that the parts of the character that are described initially by line (perhaps later to become computer generated) have a type of feel based on the weight, curvature, and clustering of line that can be anywhere from inert to literally boiling with activity. The drawings of Honoré Daumier, a French artist of the 19th century, are good examples of how the nature of the form that is described by line directly influences how we feel about the character. Mannequin-like line quality that is straight, with generic line weight and direction, gives the obvious sense of lifelessness we associate with untrained, over-observed drawings. We have all seen them, copies of photographs that have been then rendered with graphite and a stub until there is nothing left of the original life of the subject. Even preliminary line drawings done in this style leave us cold.

Take for example a robust gorilla character, roaring at the camera with obvious rage.

figure | 9-2a |

Gorilla character keyframe.

figure | 9-2b |

Gorilla character keyframe.

figure | 9-2c |

Gorilla character keyframe.

Not only is the general line of action a consideration, but also the angle of the charge, as well. Next, we observe the proportions of the gorilla. The relationship between the shoulders, torso, and head is enhanced to give us a variation in scale that is, in itself, a kind of visual rhythm. Objects scaled the same become repetitious, and in a larger context—for example, a street scene—the lack of variation of same-sized buildings and filling elements, such as carts and horses, can make our eyes move in identical jumps until we are bored. The curves used to describe the musculature of the gorilla are pushed to their limit without losing the true anatomy, and even there have variation. This variation can take the form of the curve starting more tightly and releasing in a longer arc, only to return to an almost straight line (as in a bicep). Each form is observed such that any generic feeling found in curves and their relation to other lines is minimized. In animation, especially two-dimensional traditional animation, there has to be some loss of this detailed analysis, because it is simply not possible to include so much information in each drawing of the thousands and thousands that are necessary for a feature or featurette. *Nevertheless, the basic principle of dynamism through manipulating each element and their relationship to each other and the whole character holds true. All the best characters in animation have this kind of push/pull feel in their body forms, a sort of tension built up by variation of scale and contour that still remains whole.*

Posing takes us to another realm in dynamic movement. It is entirely possible to have very quick action that is utterly dull. Often the reason is the choice of pose(s). A certain liberty may need to be taken in choosing poses, because those that are traced from real life can oddly have less dynamism than the artist can insert. This occurs because in the edited and extremely attention-focused world of animation, elements such as light, action, and pose often need to be enhanced to tell the story in a gripping way. Many examples come to mind, but reference to the few keyframes and in-betweens that follow will graphically illustrate this point.

figure | **9-3a**

Frame: arena battle, Key 1.

figure | **9-3b**

Frame: arena battle, Key 2.

figure | **9-3c**

Frame: arena battle, Key 3.

figure | **9-3d**

Frame: arena battle, Key 4.

figure | **9-4a** |

Frame: figure with tongue, Key 1.

figure | **9-4b** |

Frame: figure with tongue, Key 2.

figure | **9-4c** |

Frame: figure with tongue, Key 3.

figure | **9-4d** |

Frame: figure with tongue, Key 4.

figure 9-5a

Frame: lion roaring, Key 1.

figure 9-5b

Frame: lion roaring, Key 2.

figure 9-5c

Frame: lion roaring, Key 3.

figure 9-5de

Frame: lion roaring, Keys 4 and 5.

You will notice that torque or twist, overlap, asymmetry, size variation, and point of view all greatly improve the dynamics of a pose (and obviously, a sequence of action). These tools should be studied and used, first in still poses, and later in a series of poses (as discussed in the exercises in Chapter 4), until your characters come to life. There are, clearly, times when conservative posing is required for the sake of the story and character. You don't want a dainty ballerina to adopt the grimaces and body movements of a gorilla, and conversely, the gorilla flops as a character if it is too dainty, *unless* that was the intention.

Use of collateral aids, like costumes and props, can also enhance the dynamism of the character drawing. Each of these elements is subject to the same qualifying characteristics that were outlined above. Cloaks and other free-moving items obviously need to be studied from real sources, in the same way that anatomy should be studied. Surface texture (remember simplification?) should enhance the character and not inhibit the movement or dynamic quality of that movement.

BOUNCING FROGS

As part of the planning and layout process for rough animation, it is often helpful to create an action path to aid in placing the direction of movement animated objects and characters. An animator can make an underlay drawing for an animation sequence (placed on a lightbox beneath the animation drawings) having a drawn line or series of lines that create a pathway to show the keyframes and for blocking in the action. This pathway drawing may also plot background/scenic elements to aid in character placement.

A simple example of this type of reference would be the creation of an action path to direct the bounces of a rubber ball or a leaping frog as he jumps into the scene and hops toward the viewer.

This directional line helps to define the perspective issues related to each leap, keyframe placement, and proportional changes to the frog as he moves in space.

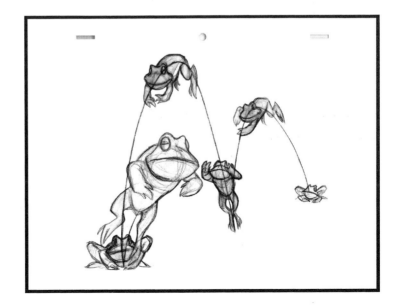

figure | **9-6** |

Leaping frog action paths.

FLIP AND ROLL, BABY!

It is imperative to check the functionality of our animation before we completely refine it and commit the drawings to their final form. *Flipping and rolling are two basic methods by which the animator can keep an eye on the progress of his work and observe the motion at work in an animated sequence. Each method involves manipulating the animation drawings like a flipbook, so that the rapid observation of the successive images gives the animator a clue as to how the filmed animation will look.* Flipping is the best method for checking the look of a completed sequence. The animator grips the animation drawings at the perforated edge of the pages (where the registration holes are located) and rolls his/her thumb across the papers like flipping through the pages of a book, getting a staccato preview of the animation.

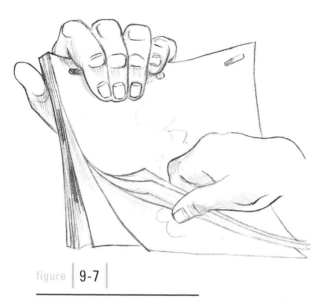

figure | **9-7** |

Flipping the pages.

Rolling is similar to flipping but is used primarily to check drawing quality and progression between two to four drawings during the creation of the animation. In this method, the animator places his/her fingers between the drawings and rolls his/her hand and fingers to and fro, checking the relationship of each drawing to another.

figure | **9-8** |

Flipping the pages.

DRAWING DILEMMAS

Most of the problems that animators face in creating rough animation are drawing-related. These problems between drawing technique and animation can be broken into several categories, including anatomy, movement/fluidity, line technique, proportional measuring, and sequential continuity. Foremost of these issues is accurate description of anatomy/proportion,

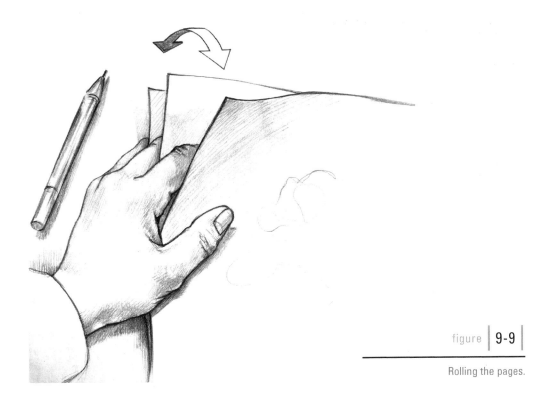

figure | **9-9** |

Rolling the pages.

followed by a dynamic, fluid drawing style. Without foundational drawing knowledge, there can be no possibility for the creation of any professional animation. One has only to compare high school sketches to the preproduction work done for a feature film to see the difference. Style—meaning the ease and dynamism in rendering figures and objects, both stationary and in movement—is a necessary skill that comes only from long practice in quick sketching. Understanding active versus passive design in the construction of poses (and backgrounds) is a field of study in itself.

Finally, continuity in action is a skill set only obtained through sequence studies of the figure. These are viable only with sound structural knowledge of the subject. Drawing skill has several parts, each important and each crucial to the success of the others. Ease in use of line is obviously critical. This, in some respects, is a hand mechanics problem. Clean, repeatable line and form are essential in constructing any good, and commercially viable, animation.

SHOOT FIRST, ASK QUESTIONS LATER

The best and final method for viewing the functionality of an animated sequence is by shooting/digitizing the frames on a *pencil-test system* (a computer and camera setup which is used to digitize single images and play them back at a variety of frame rates for real-time viewing). Flipping and rolling are excellent tools for checking 2D animation, but there is no substitute for seeing the animation on the screen. By this means, we are able to see drawing problems with timing, changes in the volume of forms, and body parts disappearing and reappearing, plus a plethora of other issues that require fixing before the animation goes through the clean-up process. Also, it should be noted that the ability to change the frame rate with the pencil-test system could allow the animation to be slowed down, thus making problems more discernable.

Back in the old days, animators had to shoot their animation tests on motion picture film, which created lag time in viewing the project due to the time required to process the film. The digital age now provides studios with equipment for rapidly creating animation tests that can be produced and viewed in a much shorter length of time.

CLEAN-UP TIME!

In this book, we've discussed the need for good gesture drawing and observational sketching skills for the animation artist, and how important it is to keep it rough and to use dynamic motion over detail. Now it's time to talk about *clean-up drawing*. The following interview took place with experts Cesar Avalos and Andrzej Piotrowski, former clean-up animators at the now-defunct Fox Animation studio in Phoenix, Arizona. Cesar and Andrzej worked on such animated feature films as *Anastasia* and *Titan A.E.* This is what they had to say…

THE INTERVIEW

Kevin Hedgpeth: "Please define clean-up drawing for animation."

Cesar Avalos: "I would define clean-up animation as the final process in animation where rough animation is made perfect. The clean-up department gets rough animation with a lot of mistakes in it, especially in regards to the meticulous details. With clean-up animation, you have to put all the details in the drawings and make sure it (the animation) runs perfectly. Yeah, it's 'perfecting the animation.'"

THE ANIMATOR
AT WORK

Bill Plympton

Born in 1946, animator Bill Plympton started out drawing and dreaming of animation in his Oregon home. By the age of fourteen, he had submitted drawings to Disney Studios, only to be told, of course, that he was too young. After graduating from Portland State University, Plympton began a career as an illustrator, and worked for such publications as *Vogue*, *Penthouse*, *Glamour*, and *The*

New York Times. He was especially well known for his quirky caricatures. His cartoon strip *Plympton* began in the *Soho* weekly news and eventually was nationally syndicated.

Bill's first venture in animation was for Valeria Wasilewski's production of *Jules Feiffer's Boomtown.* This led to *Boomtown*, his first substantial animated film, and although it did not produce much revenue for him, it was a critical success. His wonderfully sketchy, humorous style began to catch on, and a cult following started (and continues) for his goofy animation. He soon followed these early animations with *Drawing Lesson Number Two* and *Your Face.*

Seeing that his work was well received, he returned to some of his older cartoon subjects and converted some of them into animations. These included *How to Kiss,* a kind of laugh out loud surrealistic look at the kiss, *One of Those Days,* and the hilarious *25 Ways to Quit Smoking,* with absurd and outrageous solutions to the habit.

His work began appearing on MTV and at numerous animation film festivals. At this point, Plympton produced his first feature-length film *The Tune,* where a songwriter looks for creative inspiration. Part of this film got the Prix du Jury award at the 1991 Cannes Film Festival. His work expanded into animations for television commercials, which rejected some of his efforts as too extreme (but still quite funny). One of his clients was Nutrasweet.

After working on *So I Married a Strange Person* in 1997, Plympton made *Sex and Violence* the following year. Both films were oriented to a more adult market, but still carried his trademark surrealistic humor. He is currently working on the feature-length animated movie *Smasheroo*, another off-the-wall comedy.

Plympton was most influenced by such old time animators as Tex Avery and the earlier Warner Brothers and Disney animations. One interesting aspect of his animation is that he primarily does all the work himself. This is a staggering workload, and shows his amazing drawing ability and speed, reminiscent of Winsor McCay.

Bill feels that aspiring animators should attend a good professional school, such as Cal Arts, or apprentice at a studio to learn the trade hands-on. He feels that it is important to try entering various film festivals for experience and exposure, but cautions against selling your work too easily. Money is the biggest obstacle to animating, and one must be resourceful and creative to overcome this problem. Plympton is an example of an artist who did not go the traditional major studio route, but instead has forged his own animation career through original and unorthodox means. He remains one of the favorites at animation festivals across the country.

Andrzej Piotrowski: "Clean-up animation is creating the final animation drawings out of the animators' rough drawings. It is the final touch up. You are putting animation 'on model' without losing the original flavor of the animation."

(Putting an animation drawing "on model" means that the clean-up animator is making the character(s) and props in the drawing look exactly like they appear on the model sheet(s), so as to keep continuity in the animation.)

Kevin: "What drawing tools are typically used by clean-up artists?"

Cesar: "The tools we used at Fox (Animation studio) were mechanical pencils and motorized erasers. Those were critical tools. Some people still used regular pencils, but they require a lot of sharpening. We used kneaded erasers, too. We worked, of course, at tables with animation disks."

Andrzej: "We used HB, H, or my favorite pencil F. The quality of hardness of the F pencil was the number one issue with me. The reason for this choice is that you don't have to put as much pressure on the paper to get a good line as with other pencils, and you don't smudge the lines as easily as you would with a 2B or even a B pencil.

"We placed clear acetate sheets between the drawings so the graphite wouldn't come off on the back of another drawing when they were stacked."

Kevin: "Describe the process of clean-up animation. The clean-up department gets the rough animation, and then what happens?"

Cesar: "After the scene is laid out according to the director, the animators rough it all out and get the in-betweeners to finish the rough animation. That process goes through about two or three tries until they (the animators) get it right. The animators show it to the animation director and after he approves the animation, it goes to clean-up where a key clean-up artist sets the pace and cleans up the keyframes. Then he/she hands that batch of drawings to the breakdown clean-up artist who just does the breakdowns. A breakdown clean-up artist(s) or in-between clean-up artists will finish the clean-up drawing. At this point, the key artist checks all of the clean animation and shoots it (on video; perhaps with the dialogue, if appropriate), and if it (the cleaned up animation) works, he/she shows it to the director or assistant director and the director approves it (or not), and that was it."

Andrzej: "The rough animation that we got in the clean-up department could be very sketchy or sometimes it might be refined. At Fox (Animation studio), we worked very clean."

Kevin: "What kind of skill set is required to become a successful clean-up artist?"

Cesar: "You know, I think you would kind of require an 'alpha' type of personality with a big emphasis on the importance of detail. People that like drafting and creating very detailed drawings, for example. Obviously, you need the standard (human) anatomy knowledge and overall knowledge of the appearance of faces and clothing.

"You're dealing with everything in clean-up. On top of meticulous attention to detail, the most important thing in clean-up was creating the perfect line. A relaxed, calm personality allows you to execute that stroke. You're trying to make the line look as if a machine had done it with a single stroke. You need to create a smooth line with no wrinkles, jiggles or kinks in it."

Andrzej: "Life-drawing knowledge is important. Patience. Cleanliness. I think those are basic issues of the clean-up artist."

Kevin: "What about knowledge of the principles of 2D animation?"

Cesar: "Yeah, that is important in the skill set of a clean-up artist. They (clean-up artists) don't just fix drawings. They are essentially animators. Some are animators who go into clean-up because they like doing that better. They need to have good animation skill under their belt because they're finishing up the rough animation."

Kevin: "What key elements are important in being a good clean-up artist? Got any tricks of the trade to share?"

Cesar: "Wow. That's a good question. Tricks of the trade, hmm? I think you (as a clean-up artist) should draw as much as you can and sketch people as much as possible. You know, develop the life-drawing aspect of it. Also, part of it might be trying to get skill at more mechanical or technical types of drawing. Not only do clean-up artists have to clean up organic things like characters, but also rigid, mechanical, man-made objects. Anatomy and animation knowledge are very important.

"Keep up with filmmaking and video production technology because clean-up artists still have to shoot animation on videotape or whatever pencil-test system the studio is using. Be aware of digital tools, and know how to run a computer. Get those skills under your belt.

"Learn to take direction because a clean-up artist can't take it upon himself or herself to change the animation, but must perfect it as it is. Just put the rough animation on model. Don't deviate from the approved animation."

Andrzej: "The eyes and faces of characters get special attention. Facial features and the head. The rest of the body could be cleaned up with a little less careful drawings. If it isn't noticed, a problem with a coat or shoes, you can speed up production time by not fixing little mistakes. Sometimes those kinds of shortcuts are done to keep the production on budget.

"Focus on the face. It's a focal point for the audience. They're watching the dialogue. Watch the characters' eyes and the direction in which they are looking. Make sure one character is looking at another character if they are interacting.

"Line work needs to be good. Avoid lazy lines. Don't change the volumes of forms. Work to get the volumes of forms down correctly. Never, ever change the key drawings. You lose the essentials of the animation if you do that. The animators are responsible for the animation, not the clean-up artists."

Cesar: "Draw all of the time."

Gee, haven't we been saying that all along?

Here are some examples of rough animation drawings.

figure **9-10**

Rough animation drawing.

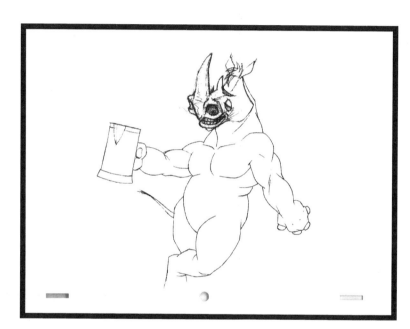

figure **9-11**

Rough animation drawing.

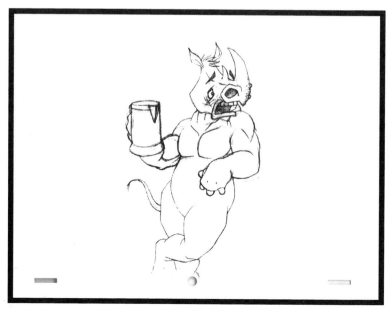

And here are some cleaned-up animation drawings from the same animated sequence.

Notice the refinement of line and character, along with the addition of necessary details (as in the costuming) in the clean-ups.

figure **9-12**

Cleaned-up animation drawing.

figure **9-13**

Cleaned-up animation drawing.

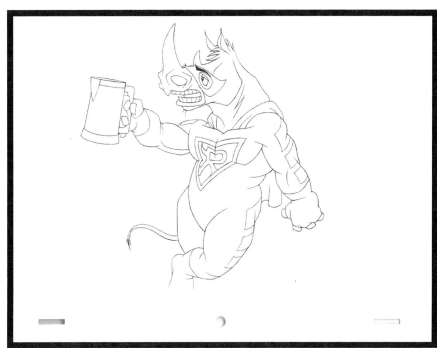

AN OLD SAYING...

There's an old adage in the drawing game that can be directly related to the clean-up and the process of drawing for animation. It goes something like this:

1. "First, you DRAW what you SEE."

2. "Soon you'll KNOW what you SEE."

3. "Finally, you'll DRAW what you KNOW."

Now, let's rephrase that notion this way:

1. "First, you carefully observe and draw from life."

2. "After a lot of practice drawing from life, you'll understand anatomy, form, and spatial relationships."

3. "Your knowledge of anatomy, form, and spatial relationships can be applied directly to your drawings without requiring live and/or outside reference."

As you work to master observational drawing from life, you will build a knowledge base of visual understanding and information about the world around you. That accumulation of information grows greater and greater as you continue to practice. This knowledge is the foundation of good drawing ability. You have to understand the structure of objects and characters to be an effective clean-up artist.

So it's obvious that unrefined skill or a lack of talent will eventually lead to problems in a 2D animated sequence. You might get away with a few bad in-betweens (assuming the key drawings are good) in a sequence, but the base level of quality will go down.

OTHER PEOPLE'S WORK

The reality of working in the 2D animation industry is that animation artists (especially clean-up animators) are predominantly going to be drawing characters and other animated phenomena that have been design by other artists. This process can present a difficult transition for animators who are not solid draftsmen/women. It is one thing to consistently draw one of your childhood character creations, but it is quite another issue to maintain continuity in design, proportion, and volume in animation when you begin to work from an unfamiliar source. The particular style of the character design can also affect an animator's ability to stay on model.

As animation instructors, we have seen many individuals succeed or fail in producing 2D animation solely based on the level of their drawing skill. So, grab a pencil and get busy.

CHAPTER SUMMARY

The importance of creating functional, gestural animation drawings as a precursor to finished 2D animation is very important. The ability to understand the concepts of the keyframe and breakdown drawings is of paramount importance in the skill set of animation artists. Building dynamic poses and understanding the application of drawing to the rough animation process have been stressed as key elements in 2D animation. Understanding and applying checking processes such as flipping and rolling to animation are necessary to the success of the 2D animator.

We also discussed the definition of clean-up in 2D animation and the importance of good observational drawing skills as related to the production of cleaned-up animation drawings. A technical drawing aptitude and draftsmanship are key elements in the skill set of the clean-up artist. The ability to effectively use outside reference (the model sheet) as a drawing key is necessary for clean-up artists.

exercises

1. Write out in simple or outline format several short scenes or sequences that can then be used for the following exercises.

2. Thumbnail a simple keyframe sequence for two or three of these scenes; draw several optional thumbnails for portions that offer clear alternative visual solutions. Remember to pay attention to the eye level, type of camera shot, and the dramatic needs of the action.

3. Turn one or more thumbnail sequences into rough keyframes, using enlargements or just by eye. Concentrate on the action, not the detail of the characters and background. Think: dynamic, crowd-pleasing, appropriate but appealing.

4. Using your thumbnails, create a storyboard for the scene being described. Note the camera shot, action, and other pertinent information below each frame. Use one frame per shot unless more are needed to explicate the action.

5. Shoot some of your keyframe sequences into mini-movies, allowing extra shots per frame, and see whether the action seems valid and successful. Alter the keyframes as needed and re-shoot.

6. Try in-betweening on one of the sequences, remembering to keep the drawing rough (extra lines are okay!). Look for continuity of motion, and try your hand at some timing. Act out the movements or videotape a friend mimicking the action(s) for use as a visual reference.

7. Choose a drawing/animation partner. Person #1 generates rough keyframes for a segment of 2D animation and Person #2 cleans them up based on a character model sheet. Check the drawings. Switch jobs and check the animation drawings again.

8. Create a set of sequence drawings from life. Retrace the drawing onto a new sheet of paper. Refine and simplify the line work. Retrace and refine until you can maintain volumes and line consistency.

9. Create a set of sequence drawings from life. Using this sequence as a reference, create a series of key drawings and clean them up.

in review

1. What is the definition of the keyframe? Flipping? Rolling?

2. What are the six planning steps in the 2D animation process, as defined in this chapter?

3. What is the definition of the breakdown drawing?

4. How is gesture drawing related to rough animation?

5. How does posing relate to dynamic movement in animation?

6. What is the definition of clean-up?

7. What are some key tools used by clean-up artists?

8. What skills are important to the clean-up artist?

index

INDEX